GEORGETOWN
Reflections of a Small Town

GEORGETOWN

Reflections of a Small Town

J O H N   M A R K   B E N B O W   R O W E

ESQUESING HISTORICAL SOCIETY

This book is dedicated to Kelly,
my understanding and supportive wife of 26 years!

Copyright © 2006 John Mark Benbow Rowe

Published by
Esquesing Historical Society
P.O. Box 51
Georgetown
ON L7G 4T1

Library and Archives Canada Cataloguing in Publication

Rowe, John Mark Benbow
   Georgetown : reflections of a small town / John Mark Benbow Rowe.

Includes bibliographical references and index.
ISBN 0-921901-28-3

1. Georgetown (Ont.) — History.   2. Georgetown (Ont.) — Biography.
I. Esquesing Historical Society (Ont.)   II. Title.

FC3099.G4R58 2006   971.3'533   C2006-902149-X

Design by Gillian Stead
Printed in Canada

The Esquesing Historical Society gratefully acknowledges
the financial support of the Ontario Trillium Foundation,
an agency of the Ministry of Culture, which receives
annually $100 million in government funding
generated through Ontario's charity casino initiative.

The 2005 executive of the Esquesing Historical Society were
Stephen Blake, President; Karen Hunter, Dawn Livingstone,
Sherry Westfahl, J. Mark Rowe, Carol Wood, Marj Allen,
Jan Raymond and Cathy Hunt.

Copies of
Georgetown: Reflections of a Small Town
can be ordered from the
ESQUESING HISTORICAL SOCIETY
P.O. Box 51, Georgetown, ON L7G 4T1
or at
www.esquesinghistoricalsociety.ca

TABLE OF CONTENTS

Loyalists wend on their way to Upper Canada.
This sketch by C. W. Jefferys brings the story of Morris Kennedy's abduction to mind. Sketch by C.W. Jefferys

CHAPTER ONE

The Kennedy Family

The story of European Georgetown and Ontario itself begins with the American Revolutionary War. When the War was concluded in 1783, American Patriots made life unbearable or even dangerous for those of their neighbours who had supported the cause of King and Country. While those who worked for the British colonial administrations fled immediately, many families remained because they had no other refuge. The Patriots began to turn their attention to neighbours who had remained neutral during the conflict, harassing them.

In British North America, the first wave of Loyalists had been settled in Nova Scotia, where a new colony was created, New Brunswick, and in Quebec where a second new colony was created in 1791, known as Upper Canada. Colonial American born Loyalists were encouraged to come to Upper Canada to settle. The Niagara District was surveyed to welcome these refugees.

Niagara District, Upper Canada was the destination of John Kennedy (1761–1847) and Charity Wurtz (1761–1800) as they travelled with their family of three boys and two girls. Their children were John (1787–1874), Elizabeth (1788–1842), Ann (1790–1797), Charles (1792–1854) and baby Morris (1794–1870). Their first challenge in the long journey was the death of their horses, forcing them to walk. Their second occurred when black-haired Morris attracted the attention of a Native woman. She nabbed the boy and ran off into the forests of Oswego, New York. Father John gave pursuit and soon returned his infant son to his distraught mother.

John Kennedy was granted land in Gainsborough Township, Niagara District in 1795. His family worked hard to establish themselves. Seven year old Ann died in February 1797, but a strong boy was born on 12 May 1797 — Samuel. He would be followed by George, born on 16 September 1799. A schoolhouse was built at Snyder's Mills (St. Ann) and John Kennedy resumed teaching, the vocation he had trained for many years before in Sussex, New Jersey.

After the death of Charity Kennedy in 1800, John remarried the same year to Barbara Slough (1773–1849) who took over the running of his household. The six surviving children welcomed their first step-brother, William in 1802. John's father and his new wife would have a total of eight children.

The War of 1812 called on the services of the Kennedy boys to defend their new home against their former neighbours. The Lincoln County Regiment, organized in 1792, was divided into five regiments. The 4th Lincoln Regiment took in the Kennedy boys. Charles achieved the rank of sergeant; John, Morris and Samuel were privates. Young George, only 13 years old at the beginning of the War, served with the Royal Artillery loading the cannons.

The boys returned safe to their home at St. Ann's to help their father support his large family. Charles Kennedy, described as a joiner, went on to learn land surveying. This decision brought him to Esquesing Township.

In 1818, the British government negotiated the final purchase from the Mississauga nation of the "back townships". His Majesty's government awarded the contract of surveying the southern part of the new townships to Timothy Street and the northerly section to Captain Abraham Nelles.

Along the north shore of Lake Ontario, west of the Town of York, lay three townships named Toronto, Trafalgar and Nelson. Three new townships were surveyed in the Mississauga tract. On 2 April 1819, the private secretary to Lieutenant–Governor Sir Peregrine Maitland, KCB wrote to the Surveyor General to order:

"I am directed by His Excellency the Lieutenant Governor to inform you that he has decided the following names shall be given to the three Townships in the Missisaque (sic) Tract now under order of survey — namely — to the western Township that of Nassagiweya — To the centre Township the name Esquesing — And to the Eastern Township that of Chinguacousy, being the Indian names of the principal rivers in each respectively."

Local tradition defines the name of Esquesing as meaning "Land of the Tall Pines". A literal native translation however comes out as "last creek out".

Timothy Street engaged a surveyor to survey the southern section of each township, in the person of Richard Bristol of the Township of Grantham. Captain Nelles engaged Charles Kennedy of Gainsborough Township, who had passed his surveying examination in May 1819.

Charles Kennedy's partial payment was 200 acres of land, which included a mill seat at Lot 21, Concession 8. His was among the first land grants approved by the Lieutenant-Governor on 9 September 1819. Kennedy married in 1818 to Elizabeth Williams (1797–1856), daughter of Benajah Williams (1765–1851) of Gainsborough. Benajah Williams was a clothier and must have given Charles a job, because he describes himself as a clothier in 1819, before he finished his surveying studies. Benajah was not only Charles' father-in-law, he was his brother-in-law! In 1805, Williams had married Elizabeth Kennedy (1788–1842), Charles' sister, and started his third family. The new Mrs. Charles Kennedy was Benajah's daughter by his second marriage.

Charles and Elizabeth Kennedy came to Esquesing in 1820 and moved into the log cabin Charles had constructed on the property beside Silver Creek. Much of his family followed. John Kennedy was granted the west half of Lot 22, Concession 8, while Samuel received the east half. Morris received the west half of Lot 20, while George moved to the east half.

John Kennedy remained in Gainsborough, selling his Esquesing property. In 1814 he had married Barbara Dean

The Town of Georgetown was named for George Kennedy, the first owner of the mill here.
EHS p110

Sarah (Bedford) Kennedy was the wife of George Kennedy.
EHS p204

(1791–1861), who went on to have 11 children. They are both buried in St. Ann's Cemetery, Gainsborough, Lincoln County, Niagara.

Elizabeth (Kennedy) Williams came to Lot 21, Concession 10 in 1825 when the village of Williamsburg was established by her husband Benajah and their sons. They had ten children, all of whom lived in the area for most of their lives.

Morris Kennedy and Sarah Travers (1795–1874) married in 1815 and brought their young family here to begin farming. They had eleven children. Morris became a minister in the Episcopal Methodist Church and was responsible for establishing the first Church in Georgetown and Glen Williams (1836). He also supported the Wesleyan Methodist Church for a time as well. With the exception of his son Morris (1824–1896), this entire family left Georgetown in 1869 for Bosanquet Township, Lambton County.

Samuel Kennedy (1897–1879) married Hannah Stull (1795–1871?) and had eight children. They remained a farming family.

George Kennedy (1799–1870) married Sarah Bedford (1798–1875) in 1821 at Gainsborough Township and moved to his grant at Lot 20 in Esquesing. The Kennedy women traveled back to Niagara District to have their children and it was then that George purchased the Esquesing lot of John Moore. Subsequently in 1823, George, Sarah, Charity and little Sarah Kennedy moved to Lot 18, Concession 8, Esquesing where George dammed up Silver Creek and erected a mill.

William Kennedy (1802–1889), son of John and his second wife Barbara, married Elizabeth Ann Travers (1804–1867) in 1824 and took up land in Erin Township. They had six children, all of whom were born in Erin Township. He was the only stepbrother to follow his older brothers and sister to this area.

A view of the Charles Kennedy saw mill operations, Wildwood Road and Main Street.
EHSp596

This beautiful Georgian brick house was built by Charles Kennedy in the 1850s. Dr. McCullough purchased the house in 1858. The residence is part of the Watch Tower complex on Highway #7 between Trafalgar Road and Main Street.
HHH 91-08-10A

Charles Kennedy built his sawmill on Silver Creek at Lot 21, Concession 8 and opened a Sideroad to link the 6th Line to the 7th and 8th Lines. His brother-in-law, Benajah Williams would continue the road (Wildwood) down into the Credit valley to his saw and gristmills. At the corner of the 7th Line and 20 Sideroad, Kennedy donated land for the first church in the Township. A Wesleyan Methodist church was built of sawn timber in 1821 to serve the Township.

Travelling south on the 8th Line, a trail led eastward to the new sawmill of George Kennedy. A small cluster of dwellings was built near the mill — the Kennedy's, the Goodenow and Garrison families lived and worked at farming and milling. Unfortunately, the business at the mill was poor, leading to the nickname of "Hungry Hollow". Kennedy added a gristmill as land was cleared to help feed his growing family.

The first child born at George Kennedy's mill was Harriet Kennedy, born 3 October 1824. She was followed by George Couse (1826), Emery (1827), Sarah Ann, Louisa (1830), John Corban (1834) and Barbara Elizabeth (1836).

Harriet Kennedy Higgins,
the first pioneer child born
at Georgetown. Mrs. Higgins
was born in 1824.
EHS p11967

The opening of the York to Guelph Road by John Galt in 1828 made Kennedy's mills more accessible to settlers and travelers. It linked the 7th Line to Charles Kennedy's mill, George Kennedy's mill and across to McNab's Mill (Norval) and onward through Chingacousy. The Road was little more than a line of tree stumps at first, but it was gradually improved.

The hamlet began to grow around George Kennedy's mills. Formal schooling began here in 1830 in the tavern, the only public building in the place. Kennedy added a foundry to the industry at his slowly growing hamlet.

Elijah Travers, Morris Kennedy's brother-in-law, established a planing mill, chair and cabinet manufactory on the east side of the 8th Line where the creek crossed the road. It grew as the settlement grew.

About 1834 at least one of four brothers working at Crook's Hollow, came to the hamlet to work for George Kennedy's woolen mill. The brothers were William, James, Joseph and Robert Barber. These four young men worked very hard and in three short years pooled their resources to buy the woolen mill from Kennedy! They would put the village of Georgetown on the map!

This benevolent view of the Mississauga at York in 1793 shows Governor and Mrs. Simcoe visiting the native peoples to celebrate the naming of York. The Simcoe dog Trojan watches while a soldier guards the entrance to the Vice-Regal residence, a tent once used by Captain James Cook.

Sketch by C.W. Jefferys based on work of Mrs. Simcoe.

CHAPTER TWO

Aboriginal Hunting Grounds

After exploring the general native history for this part of Ontario, one becomes aware that few early settlers in this area knew or even saw native peoples. They were widely spread and few in numbers. However many local people collect arrowheads and have significant collections indicating that the native peoples predate the European settlement.

These arrowhead collections originate primarily from the Credit River valley. They all date from the very ancient Huron inhabitants of this area. Hurons were a sedentary people, staying in one spot for an average of 20 years and growing beans, squash and corn, known as the three sisters. They left usually because of the depleted condition of the soil. They must have lived in the Credit valley particularly for centuries. Archaeological work based at Crawford Lake, told us a lot about their way of life and also identified hundreds of Huron village sites just along and near the Sixteen Mile Creek and the escarpment.

In this area excavations took place in 1963 and again in 1965 on the farm of Brigadier F. C. Wallace near Ballinafad, being Lot 32, Concession 10. Their analysis of the bones and bone fragments found in the middens paint us a picture of the wildlife native to this area. Evidence was found of white-tailed deer, elk, dog or coyote, beaver, black bear, woodchuck, gray fox, gray wolf, wood turtle and passenger pigeon.

Further to this, another find was excavated in 1967 in Glen Williams on Sheridan Nurseries property, roughly opposite to the former Beaumont Knitting Mills. This site was a burial pit of human remains and pottery. The Huron left their dead on raised platforms. Every ten years or so on the Feast of the Kettle, the skeletons would be gathered and buried in a common pit. If the flesh had not completely decomposed, it was the job of the relatives to scrape the bones of remaining flesh. Marks on the Glen Williams bones suggest this happened here.

The once plentiful Huron were reduced and practically wiped out by French missionaries, European diseases, and vengeful Iroquois driven by English-French rivalries by 1650. That left the region open to the Algonquian Ojibwa, who moved into this region. By coming south the Algonquians acquired rich new hunting and fishing grounds, and many obtained European names. Most frequently, in English, all newcomers in the area bounded by Lakes Ontario, Erie, and Huron were termed Chippewas or Ojibwas. The whites also used another name for the Ojibwas on the north shore of Lake Ontario: Mississaugas. In 1640 the Jesuit fathers had first recorded the term *oumisagai*, or Mississaugas, as the name of an Algonquian band near the Mississagi River on the northwestern shore of Lake Huron. The French and later the English, for unknown reasons, applied this name to all the Algonquians settling on the north shore of Lake Ontario.

The Mississauga year was divided into four seasons. Winter was called *peboon*, the season of freezing weather. Individual families or perhaps two families would hunt and trap together back from the lake, meaning the Nassageweya, Esquesing and Chingacousy area. Groups of families would gather in March at their own sugar bush to make maple sugar. This was the beginning of *seegwun*, the sap season. Then they visited the trading post and went down to the mouth of the Credit River for the spring salmon run. About the 1st of May the whole clan was gathered and they would hold religious festivals, dances and games.

The clan would then break up into smaller bands and go to their piece of lake front camp. There the women would plant corn, "when the white oak leaves reached the size of a red squirrel's foot." During *neebin*, the abundant season, the Mississauga tended their corn, ate berries, and lazed on the heights enjoying creation. At the end of the summer they harvested the corn and large quantities of wild rice from the shallow lakes and streams. With the arrival of *tuhgwuhgin*, the fading season, the Mississauga would canoe back to the Credit River for the autumn salmon run, renewing their relationships. It was at this time of the year that French traders would arrive to give buttons, shirts, ribbons, combs, knives, looking glasses, axes and blankets on credit, to be paid for in furs the following spring.

Then it was hiking to the backwoods in single file, men first, women following with all their goods on their backs. Their winter diet was dominated by meat, since hunting furs was their primary occupation. After sugaring off, they headed for the nearest trading post or paid off their credit at the mouth of the river named after the transaction.

The first purchase of land took place in 1781 by Guy Johnson. The second was in 1783 by Captain William Crawford. The largest purchase in 1784, took all land north of the Bay of Quinte and the Niagara peninsula. In 1787 and 1788, all land from the Bay of Quinte to Etobicoke Creek became Crown property. Only ten years after the first purchase, the whites numbered 20,000!

By the time Esquesing township was purchased in 1818, the Mississauga were greatly reduced and scattered. The government bought the remaining land without opposition. Since the Mississauga were nomadic, they left little behind for archeologists so we rely on history recorded by early settlers. There was a small village where the Mississauga Golf Club now stands.

The West Branch of the Credit, known as Black Creek and Silver Creek were popular with the Mississauga as quiet backwaters where they were still living when the first settlers arrived. The site of the village of Stewarttown had natives living there. They would meet there and also on Lot 18, north of Maple Avenue. Indeed much of Trafalgar Road already existed for the surveyors, since it was a Native trail leading to Stewarttown, the first village in Esquesing. The Natives stayed for the first few years until the owner of their lot showed up. In 1826, Peter Jones called all Mississauga to settle together at the

Native Canadians from the Six Nations Reserve were brought to this area to help pick hops on local farms. Their ancestors fled New York State after the American Revolution and were granted land on the Grand River. They later welcomed the remnants of the Mississauga peoples. EHS p340

Credit River Mission. Indeed, we believe Peter Jones, an ordained Methodist missionary from 1823, may have preached at Kennedy's Meeting House, erected in 1821 on the corner of Trafalgar Road and Lindsay Court. Perhaps the Methodist congregation that day included Mississauga natives who were convinced to give up their traditional life and move to the Credit River Mission, leaving the township open to unfettered European settlement.

The Credit River Mission was sold in 1847 and the remaining Mississauga Natives were removed to the Six Nations Reserve, where the New Credit Reserve was established.

The Barclay Block, later known as The Mammoth House, stands at the corner of Main and Mill Streets.

This sketch was taken from the *Historical Atlas of Halton County*, 1877.

CHAPTER THREE

The Pioneer Village

The year 1837 is a pivotal year in the history of Upper Canada and of Georgetown. For Upper Canada it marked the rebellion that shocked British authorities. For Georgetown it marked the end of insignificance. The Barber Brothers put George Kennedy's mill on the economic map of Upper Canada. The decade of the forties saw the development of the classic pioneer village. The years 1837 to 1840 were important for the growth of Georgetown.

Dissent from Esquesing Township emanated from the Scotch Block in the south of the Township. It was here that Societies were formed to suggest changes to the ruling family compact of Upper Canada beginning in 1834. On 11 August 1837, William Lyon Mackenzie himself arrived at the farm of John Stewart (Lot 9, Concession 3) for a weekend rally. Colonel Chisholm MPP came to debate with Mackenzie on Saturday. Accompanying Chisholm was Charles Kennedy. The five-hour debate was declared won by Mackenzie and the Tories left. Young John Stewart would lead a party of rebels to join Mackenzie at Montgomery's Tavern in December. He was arrested *en route*. The rebellion failed in over throwing the government.

One of the benefits of the Rebellion was the appointment of Esquesing's first Justices of the Peace. Although an appointment

had been requested of the Governor in 1821 at the Esquesing Town Meeting, it was not until 1838 that Charles Kennedy and Thomas Fyfe were appointed.

The northern half of the Township of Esquesing seemed to keep their politics at home. They played no role in the rebellion, although many came out with the Gore militia. Georgetown did not pay much attention to the rebellion because the hamlet was going through a change of its own. It was about this year that the name of Georgetown was applied to the hamlet that had grown up around George Kennedy's mills.

The most significant change was the purchase of George Kennedy's woolen mill operation by the Barber Brothers. They pooled their resources and bought the mill with the surrounding 13 acres for £750.

As mentioned earlier, Georgetown had a tavern, known as John Frank's Inn. The Esquesing Township annual meeting was held here in 1837 and 1838. Franks was still listed as an innkeeper in the 1842 census.

A general store was a luxury absent from early Georgetown. By 1837, Trafalgar Road (7th Line) had five merchants, besides their numerous taverns. Georgetown and area residents could travel to Esquesing Village (Stewarttown), the shop of William

Clay at McNabsville (Norval) or Samuel Watkins' shop at Ashgrove. Watkins' account book from 1836–1838 reveals many local names including William Barber, George Barnes, Jonathan and Hirum Bedford, Elijah Devereaux, John Frank, John, James, Thomas and Benjamin Freeman, Mark Goodenow, George Goodwilllie, Samuel, Charles, William, Morris, Duncan and George Kennedy, Jerry T. Kentner, John Kirkwood, John and George Stull, and Benjamin Vanatter. Watkins' store was on the way to Henry Fyfe's post office where the mail had to be collected from time to time.

Mail pick-up became somewhat easier in 1836 when a second Post Office was opened in Norval. William Clay (c1812–1885) was an Irish-born bachelor who operated the General Store there. He was appointed Postmaster of Norval. In 1840 the Esquesing Post Office was moved into Esquesing Village. That same year John Sumpter opened the first general store in Georgetown. Thereafter, the inconvenience of collecting mail from Norval or Esquesing Village irked the growing population of Georgetown.

On 27 April 1844, the menfolk of Georgetown gathered to sign a petition requesting a local facility. The petition, addressed to Governor Sir Charles Metcalf, estimated the village population at 200 souls. Although there were signatories from Williamsburg (Glen Williams) and

James Barber.
This sketch was taken from the
Historical Atlas of Halton County, 1877.

McNabbsville (Norval), the 98 signatures must represent almost every family in the village. The signatories include those with influence — William Barber and Ninian Lindsay, District Councillors and Charles Kennedy, J.P. Other family names include Allan, Armour, Bailey,Ball, Barnes, Brooks, Black, Bedford, Cameron, Campbell, Card, Carroll Chisholm, Clennan, Collins,Coventry, Course, Crawford, Cross, Darwell, Dobbie, Doig, Eccles, Farmer, Frazer, Garrity, Grigg, Jani, Jessop, Johnston, Kentner, Knox, Lane, Lawson, Mann, Maw, McArthur, McClellan, McEachern, McGaw, McGregor, McIntyre McLaughlin, McNamara, Miller, Newton, Nickerson, O'Reilly, Pick, Pratt, Ryckman, Scott, Sholter, Snyder, Sumpter, Sussons, Sykes, Travis, Trout, Taylor, Webster, Williams, Wilkinson, Worden, and Young. Reform Assembly member Caleb Hopkins delivered the petition. It would be seven years before the growing village received their own Post Office.

Another general store opened in 1843 at Mill and Main (8th Line) Streets. James Young (1820–1888), a Scot who had immigrated to Proudfoot's Hollow to live with his uncle, opened the store just after he married Hester Phillips.

Meantime, the village received another manufacturing boost in 1844 with the arrival of John B. Dayfoot (1813–1892). John and his brother Philo came to Hamilton from Bristol,

Vermont in 1838 to establish a tannery and a shoe factory. They decided to expand the business north into Georgetown and John purchased property on Silver Creek, which he dammed. This millpond served his tannery and the shoe factory next door. They built their house on the hill above the factory, closer to the 8th Line. In 1848, John and Rosetta Dayfoot returned to Hamilton, switching residences with Philo and Sarah Dayfoot.

On the south-west corner of Main Street and Mill Street was Young's store. On the north-west corner sat a tavern owned from 1846 by Robert Watson, known as the Balsam Hotel. Across Main Street was a second hotel, which may have been John Frank's Inn from 1836. Mr. Hatch ran it in 1846, followed by the McFeran's. Alfred Bedford purchased the old place in 1849. It was consumed by fire on 29 April 1850.

In 1848, the south-east corner was taken by Francis Barclay (1822–1889). He opened a dry goods store there with Peter MacDougald. The partnership only lasted a year, but Barclay continued to flourish.

A thriving village was evolving. A reporter traveling around Canada West for his newspaper, the *British Whig* of Kingston, wrote a flowery description of Georgetown in 1847.

Wilf Bessey stands in front of the Feed Mill on the south-east corner of Guelph and John Streets. This was George Kennedy's "Hungry Hollow". EHS p284

Oxen traffic at Mill and Main about 1850. The covered balconies of the Clark House, on the right, face the Bennett House on the left. EHS p262

C.W. JEFFERYS

Emerging from the interminable forest, you come by a short turn upon a beautiful verdant slope; another turn and you came in full view of the village, its end reposing in a valley, and laved by the crystal waters of the Credit. Its top climbs the opposite hill, which is crowned with a luxuriant maple grove. The Credit here takes the form of a semi-circle, and nearly enclosed the end of the village in an island. The whole village is enclosed by a thick bush, through which a white cottage now and then peeps. The houses are neatly built, and serve to assure you of the comfort of the inmates. The village numbers about 700 inhabitants...

The article goes on the describe the principal industries as being Travis' furniture, employing 30 hands, Dayfoot's tannery with 50 workers, two saw mills, a grist mill, an iron foundry run by John Dolson and the woollen factory with 14 looms and two spinning jennies, run by the Barber Brothers.

This large village had need of churches and Georgetown boasted three. The oldest was the Wesleyan Methodist Chapel, built on a laneway off Main Street known as Wesleyan Street. This congregation was a branch of the original Wesleyans established about 1821 on the corner of Charles Kennedy's property at Trafalgar Road. While this Church continued to serve the rural area, a new chapel opened in Georgetown village in 1841.

Ministers who carried the Bible in their saddlebags traveled through the forests of Upper Canada to preach to small and remote congregations like Kennedy's Meeting House.

Sketch by C. W. Jefferys.

It opened on 24 October 1841 with a 10 o'clock service when the Rev. John Roaf preached, followed by a service at 2 in the afternoon led by the Rev. Egerton Ryerson.

The Congregationalists organized about 1840 and met in the schoolhouse under Rev. Stephen King. James Barber joined the church and supported it for the rest of his life. They moved into the Wesleyan Methodist Chapel and met there until they built their own chapel in 1851 on Church Street. The chapel was crowned with a fifty foot spire supplied with a bell! The opening service featured Rev. John Roaf in the morning and Rev. R. Robinson in the evening. Local ministers participating included Rev. R.J. Williams of Eramosa; Rev. Hiram Denny, the pastor; Rev. M. Ritchie, Wesleyan; Rev. Heyward, Episcopal Methodist and Rev. Clarke, Baptist.

Next was the Episcopal Methodists who had opened a Glen Williams chapel in 1840 under Morris Kennedy. Kennedy gave the land for the chapel and burying ground on the Toronto to Guelph Road. A chapel for Georgetown village was erected in 1843. The trustees were Charles Williams, Henry Grass, Allen Kennedy, Elijah Travers, John Dolson, Richard Moote and Isaiah Bailey.

The Dayfoot family were instrumental in founding a Baptist Church in Georgetown. John B. Dayfoot joined the Esquesing Regular Baptist Church under Samuel Worden. Dayfoot brought his father Michael with him to Georgetown and when the

The pastoral beauty of the Silver Creek flats, upstream of Guelph Street (Highway #7), occupy the site of the original George Kennedy settlement. Postcard courtesy Dawn Livingstone.

Young Doug MacLaren enjoys his garden in front of the family home, built by James Barber in 1858. It was destroyed by fire in 1990. EHSp389

Willowbank *was the home of William Barber on Park Street.*
The main house on the left still serves as a private residence. EHS p15015

Second Esquesing Regular Baptist Church was organized here in 1847, Michael Dayfoot was the first treasurer and deacon.

In the mid-forties, Presbyterians gathered in one another's homes for visits of Robert Wallace, a travelling missionary. Although there were churches at Union, Norval and in the Scotch Block, villagers wanted a more convenient location. However, Georgetown wouldn't build its' own Church until 1867.

George and Sarah Kennedy donated an acre of land to the Church of England in 1849 for a church and burial ground. However a church was not built in Georgetown until 1855.

In order to improve the religious education of their children, a Union Sunday School Society was formed in November 1843. Charles Kennedy was appointed superintendent of the Sunday Schools while James Robertson was the librarian. The committee subscribed one shilling, three pence each for a year, the proceeds used to purchase books. The library was comprised of 120 volumes. James Barber and John Freeman completed the executive of the group.

Georgetown grew quickly in the 1840s, providing a home and a job to a growing number of villagers. As with any pioneer village, it provided just about every service that could be wanted. However, its specialties became woollen products by the Barber Brothers and leather boots by the Dayfoot Brothers. Georgetown had eclipsed neighbouring Stewarttown and now rivalled Norval in importance.

Barber Paper Mills in 1877. The home of James Barber overlooks the operation, where Stewart MacLaren Drive now runs.
This sketch was taken from *the Historical Atlas of Halton County, 1877.*

WILLIAM BARBER & BROS (GEORGETOWN PAPER MILLS) JAS BARBER PROPR.

The Georgetown Grand Trunk Station is shown about 1908. The water tower for the steam engines stands behind the station. The original stone station was built in 1855 and enlarged in 1892 after the closure of the Hamilton North-Western Station. The tower was added in 1904. EHS p315

CHAPTER FOUR

Railway Fever

The threat of Georgetown becoming the dominant village was not a prospect relished by the people of Esquesing. They were becoming worried. In 1849, David Cross, tanner of Stewarttown built a large brick hall which he planned to sell to Esquesing Township as their Township Hall. A public meeting was called to formalize the tacit arrangement. Georgetown residents invaded Stewarttown, insisted their village was a better location for the township hall, and voted the plan down. Township Councilors rented premises across the road for the next 76 years. Georgetown was not popular.

The most important asset of Stewarttown was its location on Trafalgar Road, the primary route for all trade from the lake (by ship) to Trafalgar, Esquesing, Erin and Garafraxa townships. For that reason, a Road Company was formed to plank Trafalgar Road from the lake north. The Trafalgar, Esquesing and Erin Plank Road Company was a private joint stock enterprise undertaken in 1846. Private capital was difficult to raise but enough was secured in 1850 to build 18 miles from Oakville to Stewarttown. A firm road of planks was laid across four-inch square stringers. This was completed in November 1850 and a large celebration was planned in Stewarttown Hall on 5 December. On 4 December the County Council pledged £3000 to the project. This allowed the road to be extended into Wellington County, where another £1500 was subscribed. A series of toll gates would be erected and it certainly seemed worthwhile. The trip to Oakville now took only three hours for the low toll of two shillings!

Not to be outdone, the village of Norval was working on their own plan to eclipse Georgetown! A planked road from Toronto to Guelph via Streetsville was subscribed. A "brilliant" ball was attended by 120 people in a "ball room" erected for the purpose by William Clay, postmaster and merchant. Searl's band from Toronto played for the revelers until two in the morning, when all adjourned into another supper room, "fitted up with a splendour reminding one of the Arabian Nights!" After this supper, speeches began. The supporters of this road included William Barber, William Gooderham, Francis Kent, James Menzies, George Kennedy, Philo Dayfoot, William Clay and John Miller. This local "gentry" must have arrived home when their servants were just rising!

The wonder and excitement of two planked roads were short-lived. In August 1851, a meeting was held in Guelph to organize a railway company to lay rails to Toronto from that city. The following month the group met in Georgetown and was unanimously supported at the meeting chaired by James Young with Richard Tracy taking minutes.

The Canada Directory Nov. 1851— Georgetown, Canada West

The usual stage fare from Toronto is 5 shillings; from Hamilton 3 shillings 9 pence!

Business Person	Services	Business Person	Services
W. Anderson	Boots & Shoes	J. Marshall	Tailor
Barber Brothers	Woolen manufacturers, iron founders, machinists and saw mill proprietors	H. McCullough	Saw Mill
		M. McLauchlin	Tailor
		Mrs. McLlellan	Milliner
Francis Barclay	General Merchant	Mrs. Mackenzie	Milliner
George Beswick	Boots and Shoes	J. McLellan	Carpenter
Randall Campbell	Georgetown Hotel	J. McNamara	Mason
M. Carrol	Smith	J. Quinlan	Carpenter
Philo W. Dayfoot	Tanner & wholesale boot and shoe manufacturer	John Sumpter	General Merchant and Postmaster
W. Elliott	Carpenter	Elijah Travis	Cabinetmaker
Henry Grasse	Mason	Joseph Vanallen	Tailor
J. Hardaker	Boots & shoes	James Watson	Mason
George Herod	Medical Doctor	Robert Watson	Balsam Hotel and Stage House
George Kennedy	Miller and iron founder	Henry B. Webster	Tanner
H. Kennedy	Saw Mill	James Young	Reeve, General Merchant, Insurance Agent
Rev. Morris Kennedy	Episcopal Methodist		
Elijah Leavens	Saddler & Harnessmaker		
H. Mallory	Smith		

Speculators bought up land as quickly as they could along the proposed routes. The Young and Barber families were foremost in acquiring as much property as they could. The route through Weston, Brampton and Georgetown was announced in May 1852. The effects were immediately noticeable.

Land prices shot up — not just those along the route, but heavily wooded parcels in close proximity. These trains would be burning cordwood. In fact the annual contract for Georgetown called for 200 cords of maple and beech! This made escarpment lands — worthless for farming, of relative value.

George Kennedy saw a great opportunity to make some money. In March 1854 he announced a political dinner in honour of Reform Member John White (1811–1897). It was preceded by an auction of the village lots near the railway. The lots that sold earned him from £30 to £50 each. Many lots would not be built on for decades.

The work of building the railway fell chiefly to Irish Catholic labourers. Hordes of navvies invaded the area, which sent commodity prices like butter, cheese, potatoes and coarse grains as high as downtown Toronto!

These itinerant workers were not welcome in Georgetown. They brought a "wild-west" frontier atmosphere to quiet

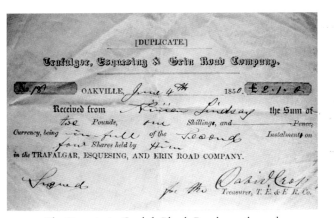

The Toronto to Guelph Plank Road ran through Georgetown to intersect with the Trafalgar, Esquesing and Erin Plank Road. Private investors paid for the planking of these roads. This receipt is for shares purchased by Ninian Lindsay on 4 June 1850. EHS p10397

Georgetown. The Irish had a reputation for carousing and drinking that was soon justified. *The Globe* of 28 July 1853 carried the headline — "Riot at Georgetown"! It spoke of a rampaging group of drunken workers who smashed up Gill's Tavern and Dr. Herod's surgery.

The news had reached Toronto — and indeed the world — in a very short time, thanks to the newly completed telegraph lines that followed the rail route. The first man to learn how to use the telegraph was Samuel Phillips, a relation of James Young's wife. He opened a telegraph office for the Montreal Telegraph Company at the back of his uncle's hardware store.

The railway added at least three new drinking establishments to the original two downtown. The Railway Exchange Hotel was opened by Robert Jones and run by John Higgins. Alex Campbell opened the American Hotel at Guelph and Main Streets, while William Higgins took over Gill's Tavern down the hill.

The coming of the railway put Georgetown on the political map. In preparation for an ensuing election, John White, the reform candidate sponsored Georgetown's first newspaper — *The Georgetown Star*, which was launched in 1852. It folded after a few weeks, right after White's election victory. S. J. Jones moved to Guelph Street to set up his printing press and he continued as a printer. Another election call resulted in the launching of a second *Georgetown Star* in May 1854. The reform paper zealously attacked opponents of the cause. When Conservative Colonel George K. Chisholm (1788–1842) won the seat, the light of the *Star* was quickly extinguished.

However, a market had been created. Four months later, *The Streetsville Review* announced, " *The Canadian Champion" Such is the magniloquent "caption" of a neat wee radical sheet, which has commenced holding forth in Georgetown. That clearing has already witnessed the quenching of a brace of typographical "stars", but perchance the Champion will be able to keep his pot boiling."* Georgetown now had a local paper to report local news.

While Georgetown prospered and suffered from the railway plans, the costs were mounting. The route chosen was projected to cost £300,000! It was hoped wooden bridges would suffice at many of the crossings, but the expanse of the Credit River at Georgetown was daunting. In the Autumn of 1854, the Toronto and Guelph Railway Company was taken over by The Grand Trunk Railway of Montreal, which had been formed in 1852.

THE NEW-YORK ILLUSTRATED NEWS.

THE PRINCE OF WALES AND SUITE VIEWING THE CREDIT BRIDGE OVER THE CREDIT RIVER, NEAR GEORGETOWN. FROM A SKETCH BY OUR ARTIST. See 2nd page.

The wonder of the "iron bridge" over the Credit River at Georgetown was demonstrated to H.R.H. Prince Albert Edward, Prince of Wales, when he passed through the village in September 1860.

The sketch is from the *New York Illustrated News.*

All the bridges were upgraded to stone. The Credit River bridge was described by engineer Fred Cumberland as the most important structure on the line. Over £25,000 was expended to build 8 spans of 96 feet each, giving a full length of 921 feet. The remaining 1000 feet were made up by embankment. Cumberland describes it, "The piers and abutments of this structure are constructed entirely of a very beautiful quality of sandstone of fine close and hard grit, and of a very agreeable warm colour. This stone is brought by tramroad from the Georgetown Quarries, four miles distant…" Although one Irish workman named Mahan fell to his death in 1854, a fine bridge was completed.

On 20 June 1856, the first train carrying officials crossed this bridge from Toronto and carried on to opening ceremonies in Guelph. Georgetown now officially eclipsed the neighbouring villages, becoming the principal town in the township overnight.

The railway brought unexpected news with unforeseen results to Georgetown. The village's leading industrialists, the Barber brothers announced that the railway made consolidation of their woolen mill feasible. They chose Streetsville, where the power of the Credit River would drive their machinery. The Georgetown woolen mill closed in the Spring of 1855. In the

The "iron bridge", built by Irish immigrant workers in 1854 was 921 feet in length. It still supports all modern rail traffic. EHS p150

The Clark Hotel sketched in 1877. The three storey brick addition was built in 1870 by Henry Tost. The original hotel with verandah and balcony was destroyed by fire in 1888 and replaced by the present brick structure of The McGibbon Hotel. Taken from the *Historical Atlas of Halton,* 1877.

meantime, however, the railway prompted a Scots immigrant, David Forbes to decide on Georgetown as the place to open a paper mill. The Barber's agreed to become his landlord and built a 100-foot stone building on the Credit River in 1854. Forbes' ambitious plans proved his undoing. He became an insolvent and the enterprise was taken over by James Barber. The papermaking era had begun in Georgetown. It would last for 137 years!

The rise of drunken behaviour caused by the building of the railway must have horrified the Barber brothers. They had worked hard to create temperate hard-working employees. In 1842 the Montreal Temperance Society had pronounced Georgetown a sober, industrious and prosperous village and they attributed it to the policy of the Barber brothers not to employ any drunkard. The "Riot at Georgetown" headline eleven years later ruined their efforts. It did attract the New York based Sons of Temperance, founded in 1842. In 1852, they came to Georgetown and built a hall at the corner of Guelph and Chapel Street. To help with the upkeep of the hall, the Sons of Temperance entered into an agreement with the trustees of School Section #10, to lease the ground floor as a schoolroom for Georgetown. The upstairs could be used as a Town Hall.

Alternate educational facilities were attracted to Georgetown as the Common School got their first permanent home. The Rev. Charles Dade (1802–1872) moved his private Anglican Academy here from Oakville in 1854. His wife, Helen Phillips, was the sister of James Young's wife Hester. Dade's students included members of the Goodwillie, Barber, Standish and Young families.

The most impressive addition to Georgetown education was the construction of a large three-storey brick facility, dubbed the Canadian Collegiate Institute, north-east of Dayfoot's Tannery. The Rev. Malcolm McVicar (1829–1904) taught at Glen Williams SS#11 in 1853 and purchased the land for his school. Construction began in 1855 and local contractor William Watson worked on it. He opened it in 1857 with Rev. Alexander Dick (1817–1901) of the Oakville Grammar School and Thomas Connell. The school opened with 78 pupils. The boarders at the school paid $42 per quarter — twice the amount charged by the Rockwood Academy! However, the "Panic of '57" depressed the economy and by 1861, the mortgage was foreclosed and the building closed.

Rev. John G. D. Mackenzie (1822–1873) came to Georgetown in 1857 to take over the Anglican parishes of St. Paul's, Norval and St. George's. He started his own private boarding Academy, which he operated until 1860 when he moved to Hamilton to run a Grammar School there.

Private primary education was also offered beginning in 1859 when Ann McMaster moved here from Streetsville and set up on Main Street, near the Congregational Church. It was nicknamed "the Old Maid's School". She operated until about 1870.

The Select School opened in Georgetown about 1865 and operated for five years under Mrs. Margaret Scott, a widow. Her references included Rev. Dr. O'Mera, Anglican successor to Rev. Mackenzie and Rev. Joseph Unsworth of the Congregational Church.

Although the Anglicans had established themselves in Georgetown at an earlier date, a Church was not built until 1855. It was a frame church with large windows, a tower with spires and square pews. It was dedicated to St. George.

The railway brought a new denomination to Georgetown, the Roman Catholics. Irish labourers planned to settle here and in 1854 purchased land on Main Street. It wasn't until 1858 that a square wooden church was built on the lot at Main Street and Park Avenue. It was consecrated to St. Patrick and was served by a visiting Jesuit priest from Guelph twice monthly.

All of these changes were occasioned by the arrival of the railway through Georgetown. The village was now on the map of The Canadas and would forever eclipse the villages that had once competed with it. The railway had also changed the definition of Georgetown. It would become known across the nation as "papertown"!

A view of Georgetown taken from the railway at John Street, about 1910.
The long building was the Dayfoot Boot & Shoe factory and has been converted into town houses. EHS p210

CHAPTER FIVE

The Barber, Young and Dayfoot Era

While the railway put Georgetown on the map, three families were largely responsible for ensuring it would remain there! By 1855, there were five Justices of the Peace. Charles and George Kennedy were the respected founders of the Village but had little economic impact. The other three were William Barber, James Young and Philo Dayfoot. These two manufacturers and merchant controlled much of the economic activity of the area, were prominent in religious affairs and represented the law of the land.

William Barber and Brothers had no formal deed of partnership, but their cooperation resulted in a prosperous business. The eldest brother, William (1809–1887) was the brother-in-charge! He was a District Councillor for Esquesing, later a Reeve and was named Justice of the Peace in 1843. It was he who surveyed and sold lots with James Young in the Park district of Georgetown. Although he built himself a house in Streetsville in 1862, he became the Member of Parliament for Halton from 1867 until 1879.

James Barber (c.1811–1880) was trained in the paper trade when James Crooks built the first paper mill in Upper Canada at his settlement, Crook's Hollow in 1826. When payment was demanded for the newest paper-making machinery from Scotland, David Forbes found he could not pay. Since the Barber brothers had constructed the mill on the Credit River in Georgetown, they found themselves in the paper-making trade. Brother James was put in charge! He quickly got the operation producing 200 pounds of paper per day!

At first paper was made exclusively from cotton and linen rags, but within four years, James built a second building and the mill became a manufacturer of paper from oats, wheat, and rye straw. Later they would use wood pulp, mostly basswood and poplar.

By 1862, the Mill went into the production of wallpaper and according to the Grand Trunk Railway Directory of 1864, it was the largest wallpaper manufacturer in North America.

In 1857–58 James built himself a new house on the hill overlooking the Paper Mill and his home on Main Street was leased as the Rectory for St. George's Anglican Church. Shortly after, Joseph (c.1816–1888) started on a new home beside his brother's home, adjacent to the GTR tracks on the 9th Line.

In 1869 the family decided to divide their interests and make a settlement. William and Robert purchased the cloth and woollen business in Streetsville, Joseph and his brother-in-law Bennet Franklin retired, and James bought the paper business in

Rev. Arthur Dayfoot touches the wall of the former office of Dayfoot Boot & Shoe. EHS p1311

Georgetown. James brought in his son John Roaf Barber to manage the premises.

That same year, the third building — three stories were added. This included the bleaching process to improve the quality of paper manufactured. By this time they produced machine-finished book paper, lithographic and label papers, coloured papers, posters and newsprint of superior quality.

Boot manufacturer Philo W. Dayfoot was a Justice of the Peace. Since the railway had divided his property, the northern portion was surveyed into village lots to provide housing for his employees. He himself built a new home in 1856 after sparks from the Grand Trunk Railway set his roof ablaze. As a leading citizen Philo supported community efforts, like the Wesleyan Methodist Missionary Society. Dayfoot, a Baptist, joined other non-members like William Barber, Francis Barclay, the Bessey family, Mrs. Goodwillie and James Young. Philo returned to Hamilton in 1859.

John B. Dayfoot returned to Georgetown in 1859 to run the Boot and Shoe Manufactory. Dayfoot's account book from 1860 to 1862 lists his shoemaker employees as John Buchanan, William Carpenter, Robert Craig, Thomas Daniels, R. Field, Michael Flynn, James Gould, James Govier, Hiram Grayham, R. Hanna, George Hayes, E. and James Kelley, James and John Lightfoot, William Little, Samuel McBratney, Angus McGilvray, John Morgan, John Newman, William Noble, Patrick Pickett, William Reid, Mr. Rogers, Mr. Russel, Isaac Taylor, James Wallace, George and William Watson.

The Dayfoot family home 1857-1975. EHS p906

In 1869, the tannery, adjacent to the millpond, was destroyed by fire. It was not rebuilt. That same year, Dayfoot opened a retail outlet for his boots and shoes. Alf Watson operated it until the shop closed in 1892.

The original flour mill carried on under Lawrence Rose while chair and cabinet maker, Elijah Travis was still in business. He was joined in the furniture trade by Charles Thayer who doubled as village undertaker. Cemetery headstones were available locally from Robert Calder's marble works or the Union Marble Works owned by Charles Miller and Edward Orr.

Water Street (now lower Park Avenue and Mill Street) was the industrial section where iron foundries were operated by George McKenzie and Thomas Rose. H.A. Race & Co. was a wallpaper and window blind manufacturer and E.C. White manufactured envelopes.

James Young had become the leading merchant in Georgetown. Besides his hardware store, he sold insurance, was a justice of the peace and was Reeve of Esquesing from 1851 to 1856. He teamed up with William Barber to survey the property now known as the Park district of Georgetown. One street was named for his wife's sister, Edith Phillips. Young also laid out a survey in Acton beside the new GTR station, naming a street in both Acton and Georgetown after himself. In 1863 a Georgetown Company of

John Roaf Barber.
This sketch was taken from the
Historical Atlas of Halton County, 1877.

militia was established under Captain James Young, with William W. Roe, auctioneer and John R. Barber son of James Barber, as his subordinates. His son Thomas took over the daily running of the store.

Across Main Street from Young was the Mammoth House, the dry goods business started by Francis Barclay in 1848. He built the first house on Edith Street in 1857 of the same brick used to rebuild his store at Mill and Main. In 1863 he took on two young clerks, James McLean and William McLeod. When McLean died in 1865, McLeod took on the majority of the daily work. Barclay was appointed postmaster of Georgetown that year, a post he kept until leaving town in 1871.

Across Mill Street was the Exchange Hotel, the "brick tavern" purchased by Thomas Clark from William Ismond in 1862. It would become known as the Clark House.

Robert Bennett purchased the Stage Hotel, across from the Exchange, in 1863. That completed the look of the four corners of downtown Georgetown in the 1860s.

A complete variety of goods could be purchased in Georgetown about the time of Confederation. Clothing was tailor-made by Isaiah and John Bailey, R. Geddes, John Rue or Miss Hardy for dresses. Thomas Cook was a barber or hair stylist! Boots and shoes were avail-

Berwick Hall was built in 1882 by John R. Barber on the site of the original Barber family home, which had burnt down. It was only used until 1918 and sat empty until 1945. It serves as an apartment building today at 139 Main Street. EHS p82

able from Henry Gane, Robert Laycock and J. Hardaker. Alfred Galbraith was watchmaker and jeweller. Photographs in Georgetown were available from the Craig brothers, Stewart Wilson or at L. L. Bennett's photograph gallery where you could also have surgery or have a tooth extracted!

Medical matters were seen to by Dr. William Freeman, Dr. Robert McCullough; Dr. Malcolm Ranney, or Dr. Williams Wright with prescriptions filled by Thomas Ruston. Robert Forsayeth, or John Livingston met legal needs.

Dugald Reid competed with Thomas Young as a hardware merchant. General goods and groceries were available from Peter Evans and John Robinson, Phillip Henderson and John McDermid, Hugh McKay, James Moore, Solomon Page or John Parker. Thomas Shufflebottom specifically sold books, stationery and musical instruments. Fresh baked goods were provided either by John Meadows or Hugh Murdock with butchers William Quinlan and John White providing the meat and poultry.

When visiting from out of town, Alfred Benham provided a livery stable on Mill Street. Village blacksmiths were Donald McKinnon while Hiram Culp and Daniel McKenzie had teamed up as general blacksmiths and carriage makers on the corner of Main and Wesleyan Streets. Culp and McKenzie did such a brisk business, they sold 22 buggies in two months in 1869 at an

The village built a fine Town Hall in 1878 with a tower for the fire bell and an auditorium upstairs. A lending library was established in the hall in 1880. It stood at Guelph and Cross Streets. EHS p109

Georgetown Public School, Georgetown, Ont.

An early photograph of Georgetown Public School (Chapel Street) built in 1869. EHS p613

average of $100 each! William Brown's carriage and wagon shop was on Guelph Street. Frank Taylor was a saddler.

Other services included Robert Long, cooper and Silas Statham, dealer in stoves, tin, copper and sheet ironware.

The culmination of the railway era came on 1 January 1865 when the Village of Georgetown was incorporated. A village Council and Reeve now ran the affairs of the place without interference from the Esquesing Township Council. The first Reeve was James Young. To be an incorporated village was an important milestone that also brought demands for improvements. A Village constable was hired and given a lock-up in the basement of the "Town Hall", which still doubled as schoolhouse and Temperance hall. Wooden sidewalks were laid, and a village fire engine purchased. Council leased the Market Square

*McKay Brothers store delivery wagon in front of 43 John Street. The house was built by James Scott about 1889.
McKay's Grocery was located on Mill Street behind the McGibbon Hotel until about 1914..* EHS p11971

for monthly cattle fairs and to host the annual Fall Fair. The Temperance faction was heard and hotel licenses were introduced. The pastor of St. George's Church, Rev. Henry Webb, began public readings in the winter of 1868. These "penny readings" (ten cents for reserved seats) raised funds to plant trees to beautify the village. Some of these trees still grace the streets of Georgetown today.

The Union Sunday School, started in 1843, continued to organize classes for the village students, but also continued their tradition of providing books for members and the children to read. John B. Dayfoot replaced P. W. Dayfoot, an early supporter, on the committee. William and James Barber were there, as was Thomas Young. George Kennedy had belonged to the Society from its inception, as had John Freeman.

In June 1866, Canadians were astounded when members of the Fenian Brotherhood invaded at Niagara. The Brotherhood was largely composed of Irish-American Civil War veterans who sought to achieve Ireland's independence from Britain by capturing Canada as a hostage. Militia units were mobilized and 40 Georgetown men were drafted into active service. Defenders were shipped to Niagara to post guard on the Welland Canal. One hundred older men formed a Home Guard to patrol the streets at night. The Glen Williams Home Guard apparently were given a free shot of strong beverage at the Hotel every time they passed on their rounds. The Georgetown volunteers returned on 20 June to a grateful Village. Reeve Francis Barclay gave the welcome speech, which was responded to by Captain James Young!

A motley crew of Halton volunteers poses in front of a studio back drop of Niagara Falls, after successfully protecting Canada from the Fenian raiders about 1868. EHS p443

*The original brick Presbyterian Church, built in 1867.
It was dismantled and the bricks were used to build
the home at the entrance to the Fairgrounds Park.
The present stone church was built here in 1887.* EHSp447

1872 they were redesignated as the 20th Halton Battalion of Rifles. They became the Lorne Rifles in 1881.

The Champion had covered local news since 1854, although the office moved to Milton in 1856. In 1866, the *Herald* was launched in Georgetown by Isaac Hunter of Ashgrove, former partner with Robert Matheson of the *Canadian Champion* of Milton. Hunter left on bad terms and started the *Halton Herald* to compete with Matheson. His attacks on Matheson were vicious which contributed to his demise. William Barber put the paper up for sale in April 1867. The Craig brothers, owners of a photograph gallery, purchased the paper and restored a balanced reporting of local affairs.

The local Volunteer Companies were formed into the 20th Halton Battalion of Infantry. A drill shed was built in Georgetown in May 1867, contracted to John Forsythe. The building still stands in Fairgrounds Park (2006). At their annual training they showed a keen interest in rifle shooting, and in

The necessity of providing school facilities suitable for an important village became obvious when the facilities became too small. George C. Dayfoot, John R. Barber, John B. Dayfoot, Francis Barclay, William W. Roe, Lawrence Rose and Dr. Starr debated the matter in March 1868. The following year a handsome two-storey brick school was built on Chapel Street by contractor Walter McKenzie. It was modelled after the newest facility in Toronto and had four rooms.

Red clay brick was also the choice of Georgetown Presbyterians when they decided to erect their own church. In

1862, James Young and Hugh McKay convinced the Limehouse Presbyterian congregation to join with Georgetown. The following year, they called Robert Ewing as their minister, a position he kept until his retirement in 1872. In 1866 they met in the home of James Breckenridge, to plan the building of a church at the corner of Main and Church Streets. It opened in 1867 at a cost of $3000.

The Baptists built their first church in Georgetown on the hill at Guelph and Main, dominating the skyline with a 126 foot spire on a English gothic style building. The stone was quarried at Glen Williams. Walter Blackwell and Henry Tost worked on the building. The church opened in 1869 and was supported primarily by the Bessey family of Stewarttown, the Dayfoot family and a large number of their employees.

The successful building phase of Georgetown was due in large part to the three leading families of the village and their relations. The Young's seized the moment and exploited it; the Barber's became the establishment, controlling village life with a nod of approval or distain; and the Dayfoot's quietly worked in the background. As this generation that influenced most aspects of life in Georgetown retired, the times changed and many newcomers began to dominate the face of the village.

Students of St. Francis of Assisi School pose under the arches of the Barber dynamo while on a hike in April 1992. The dynamo provided power for the mill two miles upstream from 1888 until 1923. EHS p1369

A train travels south on the Hamilton North Western line into the Grand Trunk junction at Georgetown.
The Georgetown train station is in the background with another train on a siding. EHS p14513

CHAPTER SIX

Georgetown Junction

The second railway through Georgetown helped define the village through to the Edwardian era. More than being a stop on the rail network, it became a junction. Although the size of the village remained constant after the second railway came through, the importance of the Village grew. Several significant events preceded the arrival of the new line in 1877. The first two marked the passing of the pioneer age, both physically and spiritually.

On the 28th of January 1870, the founding father of Georgetown died. George Kennedy was 70 years old and was buried at St. George's Anglican Church burying ground. His death marked the end of the pioneer era — the pioneers of the land and the pioneers of industry, who were now retiring. Other significant deaths of the decade included the first settler in Glen Williams. John Leslie, senior died on 10 November 1870 at age 86. While James Young had left Georgetown in 1865, his son carried on the business until August 1873, when typhoid fever claimed the life of Thomas Young.

The Barber brothers had retired but were represented by John Roaf Barber (1841–1917). Hoping for a military career, John had joined the local militia and saw action during the Fenian raids. When the brothers divided their business empire

in 1869, James Barber brought in his son John to manage the paper mill. They expanded but a recession forced Barber to negotiate a loan with the Bank of Hamilton in 1871. He repaid it within the year! He was Reeve of Georgetown from 1865 to 1875. He married Frances Barclay in 1868 and a year after her death in 1899 married Alberta Bessey.

The new decade brought a renewal of Main Street, albeit unsolicited! In the early hours of 8 October 1871, a fire began in the jewelry shop of George Kilburn. The fire spread quickly amongst the wooden buildings. The fire engine that the new Corporation had purchased in 1865, was full of woodworm holes, providing little assistance. A telegram was dispatched to Brampton, but their engine arrived too late to be of any use. Fortunately, there was no wind that morning. The "Great Fire" of 1871 destroyed S. F. McKinnon's shop, storehouse and home amounting to $18 000! Two butcher shops, Statham's tinshop, a harness shop, the Benham home, Chace's Hotel and stables were all destroyed. Damage was done to Clark's Hotel, McLeod's Mammoth House and the *Herald* offices. The Fire Company was reorganized in November!

Although it survived the fire, Travis' mill changed owners in 1872. Richard and Robertson Creelman returned to Georgetown

*Workmen watch the photographer in the colour room
of the coated paper mill.* EHS p112

A railway was needed to connect the County Town of Milton with the rest of the County. Philo W. Dayfoot of Hamilton, and his brother John of Georgetown worked to have a railway built linking Hamilton to Barrie, through Milton. The Hamilton and North-Western Railway's first public meeting at the Georgetown Town Hall was in June 1872. A By-law to grant a bonus to the Railway was approved by voters in October 1873. The results were greeted by a bonfire and celebrating in the streets of Town. Surveyors reached Georgetown in 1876, while workers laid the tracks. Workmen uncovered two skeletons on Turner's farm in the Scotch Block in July 1876, believed to have been a native burial site. Freight trains began running on the line first in 1877, passenger travel followed when the line was completed to Barrie.

In the meantime, the stagecoach provided service to Milton daily, connecting with trains and with the Erin stage. An equine employee passed on while working in April 1872. "Old Bismarck" died on the job. He was known as a faithful employee, his only fault being a habit of stopping half-way up hills for no reason.

Winter travel was by sleigh. Travelling through Town meant careful driving, giving local boys a chance to hitch a ride. The *Acton Free Press* offered a solution. "The practice indulged in by boys of hanging on behind sleighs driven through the streets is

and established Creelman Brothers as a dealer in books, stationery, musical instruments, and sewing machines. In 1876, they introduced the manufacture of knitting machines into their premises. It proved so successful that they pulled down the old saw mill in 1881 and built a three-storey factory on the site.

a dangerous amusement, especially in the more frequented thoroughfares. The driver who "whips behind" does the proper thing."

The Council was busy improving the village. A new hook and ladder wagon was purchased after the great fire. A proper lock-up was installed in the basement of the Town Hall and constables were hired. John Harley and John Hayes were two of the village constables. Funding for planting shade trees was given by the Council to improve the village. By 1877 the Temperance Hall / Town Hall was described as "a shabby looking frame building, situated on Guelph Street, with a lock-up in the lower storey, used principally for lodging tramps." A fire in March 1878 destroyed the building. Council initially purchased the Market Square at Church and Market Streets, but decided to build a two-storey brick hall with a hose and bell tower at Guelph and Cross Streets, directly across from the former Town Hall.

The coming of the Railway and growing prosperity of the place, induced the Bank of Hamilton to open their first Halton County branch here in 1875. The brick building was built across from the Presbyterian Church on Main Street.

Fire was not the only threat to people at this time. Spring floods, especially at Glen Williams were often annual affairs. However, disease was the dreaded killer. Smallpox was always feared, but an epidemic in 1872 prompted Council to build a Smallpox Hospital outside the village where people were quar-

The tellers take a moment at the Bank of Hamilton on Main Street, Georgetown about 1920. The Bank was part of the McGibbon Hotel block at this time. EHS p196

antined. The idea was to remove the threat to people coming into the Town to shop. The hospital burned down in 1875. One victim was Alexander Chase, the bus driver from Clark's Hotel. Typhoid fever outbreaks took lives and one diphtheria epidemic in 1876 took four children from the same family!

Percy Maw (1891-1975) poses for the photographer. EHS p1241

The decade of the Seventies saw a rise in social activities for the people of the village. Sports were patronized by leading men of the village. Dr. Standish was president of the Lorne Lacrosse Club. The Georgetown Silver Stars played baseball against other local teams. Thomas Costigan was the local umpire. Cricket, quoits and curling were organized annually.

Horse racing on the Norval Road was a favourite pastime. It was part of Queen Victoria Day activities, Dominion Day celebrations, and the August Civic holiday. The "big" event was the 24th of May which included Calithumpian parade, races, fireworks and a bonfire. Dominion Day was often an organized *picnic* or strawberry social. The Esquesing Fall Fair was a popular annual event, especially after 1877 when they used the "market square". A monthly cattle fair brought many people to the village to shop.

A dramatic club presented plays at the Town Hall. The Mechanic's Institute, which held many books in their library also organized social evenings. Five-cent readings were offered in the winter months to explore new literature. Reserved seats were available for the "aristocrats" at ten cents! Concerts at the Town Hall were very popular and always featured the Georgetown Brass Band. Some presentations included Jennie Fraser, the Wellington Warbler; the Townsend Family; Miss White of Georgetown and the Slave Cabin Singers.

The rise in organized societies was remarkable. A new meeting room was opened in 1870 at Clark's Hotel with a supper and a ball. The Masonic Credit Valley Lodge organized that year and met in this new facility. Officers included W. B. Duncan, Solomon Page and Dr. Starr.

In March 1873, six organizers opened an International Order of Odd Fellows lodge at Georgetown. Their primary mission was to help members with sickness, death and funerary expenses. The organizers were J. O. Campbell, Henry Tost, Isaac Clark, William George Lee, D. C. Watson and Robert McMaster.

A year later the Royal Black Preceptory #314 Georgetown was organized. D. C. Watson, G. C. Mackenzie and P. T. McCallum led this Orange lodge.

However, this was the age of the Temperance Society. The Georgetown Sons of Temperance had organized in 1852 and built the "Town Hall", which was burned in 1877. They were still active and competed with the Good Templars. The International Order of Good Templars was founded in 1851 in Utica, New York and renewed their efforts after the American Civil War. They held their second annual meeting for Halton County at the new Glen Williams Town Hall in January 1873. St. Patrick's Church also organized a Catholic Temperance Society with John Bird as president.

When a new elementary school was being discussed, the vacated Canadian Collegiate Institute was considered. It was used as the home of William Hope, brother-in-law of James Barber. However about 1870, the school reopened as the Georgetown Academy under Donald MacDonald (1840–1935)

Hugh Livingstone of Livingstone's Bakery poses with locals in front of his delivery wagon in 1919. Heather's Bakery carries on the tradition in the same building, although it was The Herald *office for years.* EHS p438

and Duncan McTavish (born 1839). Their students included Fred W. Barber, Thomas J. Godfrey and John D. McPherson. The institution changed hands for the Autumn term of 1872. John W. Tait became Principal and was joined by A.D. Campbell, M. McCormick, Mr. and Mrs. F. Dunn. The facility closed in the Autumn of 1875.

A view of Guelph Street showing the High School on the left, the Anglican rectory at centre and St. George's Anglican Church at right. Silver Creek runs under the road. EHS p614

The doors opened once again on 8 September 1878 under Rev. Nelson Burns. Burns had been the principal of the Milton Grammar School from 1868 until it closed in 1874. He was also the owner of the *Halton Herald* at one point. He lived here with his family and mathematics master H. A. Thomas. The fee for tuition was $5 per quarter. Students included H. Richardson, R. Higgins, T. Harrison, J.W. Stutt, Jennie Harrison and Mr. Locke. The school continued until Easter 1882 when the facility closed its doors.

In the meantime, the citizens of Georgetown began to push for a High School of their own. The Education Act of 1871 transformed Grammar Schools into High Schools. In 1886, the first Georgetown High School Board was created. The trustees were John R. Barber, Dr. Roland, Rev. W. G. Wallace, Charles Ryan, Lachlan Grant, and A.C. McKinlay. They decided to open in January 1887 under the tutelage of Malcolm S. Clark and Edward Longman. There would still be a small fee of $5 per annum for students to pay. It had been decided at the outset that school would meet in two rooms of the Public School (Chapel Street). This would force the Junior department of the school to move to the Town Hall across Guelph Street. The school opened with 60 pupils.

Once the High School opened, work began to secure its own building. Mr. Heartwell sold 3 1/2 acres for $2000. Edward J. Lennox, architect of the new home of John R. Barber, Berwick Hall was also prevailed upon to design the new High School. Lennox also designed such Toronto landmarks as Casa Loma, Old City Hall, King Edward Hotel and Massey Hall. Peter Laird and John Maxted of Norval were the local contractors. The brick architectural gem was completed in October 1889. *The Brampton Conservator* described it as, "One of the finest school buildings in this province." By 1893, the staff had doubled to Alexander Gibbard, A. E. Coombs, Miss Hagan and Miss Wright.

The original Georgetown High School, designed by Edward Lennox and built in 1889. It was demolished in 1959. EHS p640

The availability of books for public use was important to the people of Georgetown beginning with the establishment of a Sabbath School library in 1843. The Mechanic's Institute established a more practical collection in the 1850s. This collection was probably destroyed in the Town Hall fire of 1878. John R. Barber reorganized the Mechanic's Institute and their library in 1880 in the new Village Town Hall. Only members, who paid a membership fee, were allowed to withdraw books. However, the rising free library movement resulted in the collection being turned over to the Corporation in 1895, as the basis of a free lending library for the use of all citizens of Georgetown.

The small Hamilton and North-Western Railway station was just west of Main Street where the line crossed the GTR line. It traveled parallel to Main Street until it reached Wildwood, where a trestle took it across Silver Creek and across the fields towards Terra Cotta. The Western Hotel, run by George Gibbs, on Main Street North faced the tracks. In 1892, the junction was moved east so that the GTR station served both sets of passengers. The limestone station was enlarged, with the marshalling tower being added in 1904.

The Bell Telephone Company of Canada opened their first office in Georgetown in 1884 at J. H. Jackson's stationery and furniture shop. Only three of the first 16 telephones were residential. They belonged to John R. Barber, of the paper mills; Joseph Barber, retired and George S. Goodwillie, solicitor.

Georgetown Sunday School picnickers gather at the station for their annual outing to Burlington Beach about 1908. EHS p316

In 1888, John R. Barber generated electricity from his own power plant, transmitted it to his paper mill and had the first factory in North America running on electricity transmitted over a distance. He dammed the Credit River between the Paper Mills and Norval and built a generating plant and then transmitted the power over two wires up the Credit valley to his Paper Mill.

The wonder of electric lights came to Georgetown in July 1891. Joseph Williams of Glen Williams fitted his former saw mill with a water-driven generator and sold the power to Georgetown. A huge arc lamp was suspended over Main Street. Electric light was only available for a limited number of hours unless one applied for an extension for a special event. In the meantime, the Village constructed a reservoir at Silver Creek village, ran pipes down the 8th Concession and in December 1891, Georgetown had running water and the best fire protection they had ever had! Joseph Barber headed the committee which built the 400 000 gallon reservoir.

This prosperous era saw the renewal of the village church structures. The Baptist Chapel of 1869 dominated the skyline and set the tone for improvement. The Wesleyan Methodists were appropriately the first to renew their historic structure. In 1877 a modest brick chapel was built for the congregation. Joseph Barber Sr. laid the cornerstone for a new Congregationalist Chapel on Church Street in September 1877, which opened in February 1878. In July 1878, George Elliott of Guelph laid the cornerstone for a new stone Church of England with a Norman tower. Under the leadership of George H. Kennedy, the Episcopal Methodists constructed a brick gothic structure with twin towers. One tower was surmounted with a soaring steeple while a dome sat on the top of the second. This new Church opened in 1880. St. Patrick's Catholic Church was in a very bad state of repair and plans were made to replace the small frame building. It was decided to build a simple stone Church on Guelph Street, closer to the Catholics, who tended to live close to the Railway. In July 1885, Bishop Carberry traveled by train to Georgetown to lay the cornerstone for a church dedicated to the Holy Cross, with St. Patrick as a secondary saint. Knox Presbyterian Church was the final renovation on the block. The brick church was dismantled and used to construct a home at the entrance to the Park. Joseph Barber and Lachlan Grant were appointed to solicit subscriptions. Work began in 1887 on a Gothic stone church with twin towers and was completed in 1888 at a cost of $15,000.

The idea of Protestant denominations working together had been a reality in Georgetown since the creation of the Union Sunday School. However, in 1884 the Wesleyan Methodist Church and the Episcopal Methodist Church united, forming the Methodist Church of Canada. They decided to sell the chapel on Wesleyan Street and met in the brick St. John's Church on Guelph Street.

The Salvation Army marked its' local beginnings in Acton in 1884. Shortly afterwards they moved on to Limehouse and then Georgetown. They first met in the skating rink shelter, which was rather dingy, and where they were met by drunken stone throwers. The Lord's Army persevered and they moved into an abandoned brewery, dubbed the "Hallelujah Brewery". The Army was anxious to show that they could save people who felt excluded

Wilber Lake was a popular place to canoe in summer and play ice hockey in winter.
It was drained about 1915 when the Radial Railway was built. EHS p629

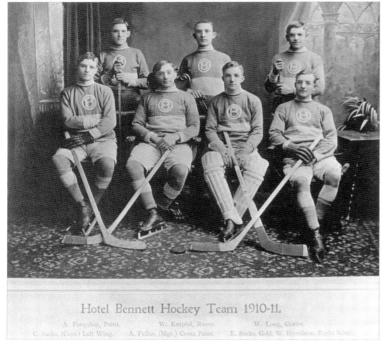

Hotel Bennett Hockey Team 1910-11.

A. Farquhar, Point.   W. Knipfel, Rover.   W. Long, Centre.
C. Sachs, (Capt.) Left Wing.   A. Fellar, (Mgr.) Cover Point.   E. Sachs, Goal, W. Hurtlee, Right Wing.

Georgetown's Hotel Bennett Hockey Team played on Wilber Lake in 1911. The team consisted of A. Farquhar, W. Knipfel, W. Long, Captain C. Sachs, Manager A. Fellar, E. Sachs, goalie; and W. Hurtlee. EHS p502

from other churches because of their poverty. The immediate response was gratifying, but the poor were not lasting adherents and drifted away. A survey of the Census records shows that the adherents were mostly labourers and servants. The Georgetown Corps closed in 1891 and was revived briefly from 1927–1936.

By the turn of the century, Georgetown was a bustling town serviced by two train lines, and serving as a centre for the surrounding rural areas and hamlets. Life was decidedly easier within the village. The village provided a constabulary, fire protection and a public library. Some people had electric light, running water and the telephone.

Everyone had leisure time on Sunday, due to the strict observance of the Lord's Day. Young people enjoying boating on Wilber Lake (formerly called the mill pond), followed by a picnic on the shore. In colder months, the "lake" was a great ice surface for hockey and leisure skating. Someone would bring a gramophone and wind it up to provide music. Edison gramophones were first displayed at the Bennett House in 1892.

Special events were celebrated by the entire community. Fall Fair day and the Queen's birthday, May 24th were heartily extolled. Added occasionally were celebrations on July 1st, and the Drummer's Snack, when travelling salesmen of Ontario would often have their annual picnic at Georgetown. These occasions often involved horse racing, athletics, a parade, and a band concert. The 1912 "Snack" of the Commercial Travellers' Association was held July 19th and 20th. It featured a minstrel show, concert and fireworks on the Friday evening followed by a baseball match, calithumpian parade and athletic games.

Other leisure time occupations were offered in Georgetown. The Royal Oak Loyal Orange Lodge started in town in 1882. The education and training of women at home was addressed in 1897 when Adelaide Hoodless created the Women's Institute. The Georgetown branch was organized in March 1903 at the Georgetown Town Hall with Mrs. L. L. Bennett as the first president.

In 1900, the Imperial Order of the Daughters of the Empire was formed in Montreal to promote British institutions and also to promote children's and community issues. A branch opened here. The Farmer's Institute, which met at the Town Hall, turned into a training session on new methods of farming.

The Boy Scout movement started in England in 1908 by Robert Baden–Powell, was first organized here in September 1910 under former High School teacher L. R. Halnan. They attended the rally at the Canadian National Exhibition on September 6th in honour of the visit of General Baden–Powell. They were often seen marching in local parades thereafter in uniforms carried by Adams and Company at Mill and Main Streets.

The ability to perform music became very important during this time and lessons were advertised by Edith Maw and Arthur B. Castell. Mr. Castell was the choirmaster at Knox Presbyterian Church, the Bandmaster and was hired by the Georgetown Board of Education to provide music classes. Georgetown Public School was a pioneer in this area.

The prosperous industrial base of Georgetown encouraged entrepreneurs in the new century. H. P. Lawson, owner of the Stewarttown saw and flour mills purchased the Georgetown saw mill. In 1897 he built a planing mill on James Street. He sold this in 1909 to an Acton sawyer, John Boyd Mackenzie (1876–1947). John and Eliza Mackenzie moved to Georgetown from Acton in 1915 and lived at "The Birches" (75 Mill Street). The Mackenzie family were responsible for many of the present buildings in Georgetown.

Another Acton businessman was Herbert T. Arnold (1858–1937) who expanded his glove factory to Georgetown in

Staff of the Bennett House Hotel takes some time out of their day for a portrait, about 1903. EHS p8529

1901. He built his new three-storey factory at Guelph and Mill Streets (Carpet Barn in 2006) and operated here until 1922, when the business was consolidated in Acton. Herbert and Melvina Arnold purchased "Grandview House" from the Goodwillie estate in 1906 and lived on Queen Street until 1932.

Thomas Speight was from another Acton family. He opened the Georgetown Electric Works in 1897 where he manufactured dynamos and motors. He took over the wiring of homes from the Electric Light Company in 1906 and provided small engines to many local businesses. In 1914 he went into motor car sales. His son Arthur continued the business until 1945. Both men were very involved in local politics.

Staff poses outside the newly enlarged Willoughby's Livery Stable about 1906. The Mill Street building served as a bakery, the liquor store, Hewson's Garage and the Royal Canadian Legion. The Legion and C&S Printing share the building today. EHS p242

John A. Willoughby (1876–1964) purchased the livery stable and bus business from H. A. McCallum in 1901. Willoughby became an active politician in Georgetown in 1904 and campaigned vigorously for a thriving town. In 1906, he had J. B. Mackenzie enlarge the livery stable on Mill Street.

The Thompson and Barnes farms were purchased by John Willoughby in 1914 and 1915, respectively. Willoughby began work to convert the land into a golf course and a trout hatchery. Before long, Cedar Crest Golf course opened at Maple Avenue and Trafalgar Road.

Harley–Kay Knitting Machines Company opened in 1906 on Water Street. Fred Harley was the son of John Harley who was a blacksmith and one-time village constable.

Donald McIntyre (1874–1934), a Scottish born florist, came to town in 1911 after serving as head grower at Casa Loma. He joined Samuel Kirk to operate the Georgetown Floral company. Their nine acres supplied flowers to Montreal, Toronto and Hamilton. The office was at 46 King Street.John R. Barber joined in this industrial boom in 1905 by opening a paper coating mill beside the railway yard. Canada Coated Paper Mills were opened under Michigan native, Edward Fleck (1882–1961). J. B. Mackenzie poured the reinforced concrete building. The Barber Paper Mills and Canada Coated Paper Mills were united as one limited company in 1911. In 1910, Fleck left the employ of Barber and, joining with John Willoughby, founded Georgetown Coated Paper Mills across from his former employer. Georgetown's reputation as a paper town was firmly rooted.

This new industry attracted the Merchant's Bank of Canada in 1905. In 1918, they purchased the site of the Coffen House (Bennett House), destroyed by fire, and built a modern building (The Old Bank).

Samuel H. McGibbon (1865–1940) moved to Georgetown from Acton in 1895 when he leased the Clark House in partnership with his brother John of Milton. The name was changed to the McGibbon Hotel, a moniker it still carries. McGibbon had a farm south of Stewarttown which provided fresh produce and eggs daily and helped him attain a reputation as a first-class establishment. Two children of Sam and Ann McGibbon, Gladys and Jack took over running the Hotel until 1962.

George Stewart Goodwillie (1842–1905) married Annie Barber and became a lawyer in town in 1876. Two years later he became the Clerk and Treasurer of the Village, a position he maintained for many years. He built "Grandview House" on Queen Street in 1880 to raise his four children. The fine house had 28 rooms, tennis courts and bowling greens. It was sold to Herbert and Melvina Arnold in 1906.

The Georgetown Herald took on a new foreman in 1891, Joseph Moore (1872–1939) another Acton boy. Moore became first a partner and then owner of the *Herald*. He married Amy Clarridge in 1896 and they made their home in Georgetown. In 1911, J. B. Mackenzie built them a fine home at the corner of Park and Charles Streets.

The 1911 census revealed Georgetown's population at 1574 persons. Although the population had grown slowly, the advantages of living in Georgetown had improved greatly over the past forty years. Businesses were thriving and manufactures

Celebrants gather in front of a festooned Hotel McGibbon during a Drummer's Snack. EHS p245

were booming. The more prosperous merchant class had every luxury found in a city. Large houses, large incomes and plenty of servants were the way of life for the few, while many scrambled to climb the social ladder, a privilege not allowed in the old country. No one could have foreseen how drastically this world was to change!

MAIN ST., GEORGETOWN, ONT.

The Baptist Chapel spire on the hill dominates Main Street.
The McGibbon Hotel dominates the right side of the street, and the Bennett House, with its balcony, is across the street. EHS p444

CHAPTER SEVEN

Old Empires and New Realities

The two world wars and the Great Depression took its toll not only on the British Empire, but on Georgetown's local empires. As the days of Imperial glory faded, so did the era of wealthy businessmen who controlled the Town's economy and its politics. New entrepreneurs stepped in.

The rising prosperity of Georgetown throughout the last quarter of the 19th century, reflected the rising pride all Canadians had in their country as a Dominion within the Empire. When the Boer War broke out in South Africa in October 1899, we were ready to demonstrate our loyalty and ability to fight along side our British brothers. Although Canada did not send an official contingent, volunteers were transported overseas by the Canadian government and were put under British officers. From the local 20th Halton Battalion "Lorne Rifles", eight men volunteered. The only local man was Lieutenant James Ballantine (1876–1948), Georgetown, with D Battery, Guelph Division, 2nd Contingent. The Village Council granted $25 as a testimonial to Lieutenant Ballantine. The 20th Halton Rifles were represented at the coronation of King Edward VII by Sergeants W. J. Gould and Beatty. The end of the Boer War in 1901 was a great day for Empire!

It was that excitement which prevailed among the youth of Georgetown in 1914 as the Balkan Crisis unfolded and the prospect of another glorious war for the Empire loomed closer. On 4 August 1914 Canada joined the war against the Kaiser of Germany. The first to volunteer in Halton was Major Frank Herbert Chisholm, a man too old to serve, but he represented the enthusiasm with which the War was embraced. The Peel Regiment and Halton rifles initially sent 16 officers and 404 other men. They became part of the 4th Battalion of the Canadian Expeditionary Force. Local chapters of the Red Cross and the Patriotic League were quickly organized.

James Ballantine was given temporary command of the 4th Battalion of the Canadian Expeditionary Force and was wounded in both shoulders. Georgetown followed his condition with interest. In May 1915, King George V received him at Buckingham Palace and awarded him the Distinguished Service Order. When he returned to Georgetown, a crowd of 2000 greeted him at the train station. A large procession headed by the Glen Williams band, school children, the 20th Regiment band, Boy Scouts and members of the 4th Battalion marched to the Georgetown park for a gala reception. Ballantine drove in the automobile of Reeve Edward Fleck. The crowd was addressed by Reeve Fleck, Joseph Beaumont, Colonel Noble and

White pith helmets mark the military band as it plays on the platform of Georgetown Station in June 1908.
Every spring all militia volunteers would be trained at the annual camps.   EHS p314

Rev. A. B. Higginson. After a short recovery, Sir Sam Hughes offered Ballantine the command of the 76th Battalion, which trained men at Camp Borden.

The Ontario Temperance Societies were finally successful in 1916 when Prohibition was introduced. What a hard swallow that would have been for returning servicemen! The ban lasted until 1927.

The Toronto Suburban Railway was purchased in 1911 by Sir William Mackenzie and Sir Donald Mann, an Acton boy. He immediately surveyed a route from Toronto to Guelph and work began in 1912. As the construction approached Georgetown, the famous Wilber Lake was drained so that a 96 metre wooden trestle could be built across Silver Creek, behind St. George's Anglican Church. The Georgetown station and electrical sub-station was built at 29 Main Street (currently the site of TD Canada Trust). When the track was being laid near the present Remembrance Park, a locomotive slipped off the rails into the heavy mud. It was extracted with difficulty. Financial troubles slowed construction down considerably, so it wasn't until 14 April 1917 that the line opened, providing electric train service from Toronto to Guelph. It was fast, quiet and non-polluting. Anyone could flag it down and get a lift along the line.

The final year of the war saw the destruction of the *Georgetown Herald* by fire in April 1918. The alarm was given by Miss Norma Millar and the telephone operator, who ran up the

Colonel Ballantine, after being injured, returned home to admiring crowds at Fairgrounds Park in 1915. The World War One hero went on a campaign to recruit volunteers. The Georgetown Armoury stands in the background. EHS p954

street to ring the fire bell at the Town Hall. This allowed the fire Brigade to save the adjoining properties. Editor Joseph Moore never missed the next issue however, thanks to hard work and the presses at the *Acton Free Press*. H. P. Moore, was only too happy to help his former employee, now editor of the Georgetown paper.

Members of the Georgetown Boy's Band pose in their new uniforms in 1920. Bandmaster Parrot stands with buglers Norm Marchment, Winston "Curly" Wheeler, and Ab Reeve. EHS p57

In October, the area was hit with the world-wide scourge of the "Spanish" Influenza. About 200 townspeople became ill. Dr. Nixon (1871–1918), Esquesing Medical Officer of Health, was the first fatality, followed by seven others. Churches and schools were closed for three weeks, reopened and closed again in January when the 'flu reappeared. The second local wave of the epidemic occurred after the December Guelph Winter Fair went ahead. Many local people attended and became sick shortly afterwards. This 'flu bug was highly contagious and struck at people in the prime of life, aged 20 to 40. The disease killed about 1,750 Torontonians.

Peace in November 1918 brought renewed optimism. Housing was in short supply, which sparked a building boom. John Ballantine and John Willoughby were credited with building many beautiful homes in town. Provincial Paper and Georgetown Coated Paper both expanded and a new industry — Smith and Stone had opened. Main Street was paved in 1920. The new Chamber of Commerce, headed by Edward Fleck reported all of this great news! The 1921 census reveals that Georgetown's population climbed to 2,061 people, which qualified the corporation to declare itself a Town. Radios, motor cars, and movies were popular. Actually, Georgetown had enjoyed movies since 1910 in the old Wesleyan Church. In 1928, Russell Gregory built a new movie house which served Georgetown until a fire in 1958. Power, provided by Ontario Hydro since 1913, was being installed everywhere under the direction of hydro superintendent Ben Forster, as electrical appliances became the rage.

Smith and Stone were formed to take advantage of the demand for electricity. Founded in 1919 to manufacture wiring devices, the new company purchased the "glass gardens", a large greenhouse operation which had recently closed. Henry Smith (1868–1947) and Benny Stone (1882–1962), tailors during the

Knox Presbyterian Church was gutted by fire in 1901. The 1885 stone church was immediately reconstructed.

Photograph courtesy Knox Presbyterian Church.

War, represented the spirit of the twenties! They operated the business successfully, selling in 1944 to Duplate Canada.

The collapse of the Ottoman Empire was signified locally with donations to support orphans from the Armenian massacres in Turkey. Relief funds were gathered, and in 1923 fifty Armenian orphan boys arrived in Georgetown to begin a new life. The Armenian Relief Fund selected Cedar Vale farm, part of the property of William Bradley as the new home for the boys. Another 40 boys arrived the next year. They were trained as farm workers and were apprenticed to farmers when they reached 18 years of age. The boys attended a different church in town each Sunday and enjoyed the YMCA summer camp above Norval. The farm school was closed in 1927.

Georgetown officially remembered the 34 men who had not returned from the Great War with the unveiling of their memorial on 24 August 1924. The war memorial was located at the junction of Guelph Street and Main Street North. The Great War Veterans Association was generously supported and organized many fundraising events. It became the Canadian Legion after 1926. Arol O'Neill headed the Legion when they moved into rooms on Mill Street in 1933. President Gordon O. Brown purchased a portion of the former Willoughby's livery stable in 1936.

When Wilber Lake was drained, Georgetown lost their best skating rink. An indoor arena was erected in 1923 by a private

Sir Arthur Currie unveils the Georgetown War Memorial at Guelph and Main Streets in 1924. EHS p39

company, led by the Georgetown Odd Fellows. The Odd Fellows meeting room was located in the arena, since their rooms were destroyed by the 1922 O'Neill block fire. The Memorial Arena was built behind the Buck family home (39 Guelph Street) where the abattoir for the village butcher was located. The Buck family ran a butcher shop on Mill Street from 1881 until 1972.

The Armenian School property was sold to the United Church of Canada and they prepared the property to receive girls who did not have homes of their own, or who could not stay at home. It opened officially on 18 May 1928 with superintendent Jessie Oliver and eight girls. As the number of girls grew, Cedar Vale School became known for their Christmas musicals and their summer garden party. They were very much a part of the community. Miss Oliver retired to Toronto in 1944.

As the Armenian Boys School closed in 1927, another farm school opened on the adjoining farm owned by Morris Saxe. Morris Saxe (1878–1965), a Russian immigrant, first opened a creamery business in Acton after graduating from the Ontario Agricultural College. In 1917, he opened a larger creamery in Georgetown and moved his family here. With his own money, he helped Jewish immigrants into Canada. The demand for farm labour encouraged him to create the Federated Jewish Farmers of Ontario of which he was president. They opened the Canadian Jewish Farm School on the 8th Line at 15 Sideroad. It opened in June 1927 with 38 Polish orphans. The school trained in market gardening, poultry raising and dairying. It operated until 1931.

The Memorial Arena was built in 1923 by a private company which operated it for twenty years until selling it to the municipality. EHS p8527

The simple pleasures of gardening became big business for William Bradley (1886–1952) when he opened the Dominion Seed House in 1928, after dabbling with electrical appliances. The mail order seed business soon spread across Canada and flourished. In 1937 he opened new mail order offices in the expansive building which immediately became a Georgetown landmark.

The first dairy in Georgetown to offer pasteurized milk opened in 1927. William Thompson(d.1934), a Norval farmer, built his milk plant at Mill and Back Streets and called it Maple

The youth of the village gather on the grandstand for a school photograph in 1921.
The Historical Society has identified 40 of the children. EHS p119

Employees at the "lower" mill pose for the photographer beside the rough stone walls of the former Barber Paper Mill in 1933.
Provincial Paper closed the "lower" mill in 1947. EHS p215

The electric Radial Railway closed the Georgetown station in 1931. The building, shown here, was taken over by Irwin Noble for his Georgetown Dairy. Noble used horse and cart to deliver milk until 1959. EHS p218

Georgetown Creamery in 1920 owned by Morris Saxe. It stood on Guelph Street by Silver Creek, where "Hungry Hollow" began! EHS p221

Leaf Dairy. He opened in competition with William Gillman of Glen Williams, who started delivering milk in town in 1920, as Georgetown Dairy. Gillman had competed with Percy and Harold Cleave, whose family had supplied milk to Georgetown since about 1910. When mandatory pasteurization came into effect, the Cleave family switched to wholesale.

The Maple Leaf Dairy was famous for its ice cream, which was very popular on Saturday evenings. This building later became Steen's Dairy Bar and is now Kentner's Catering.

Hyman Silver (1889–1951), a well-known local clothing peddler, opened his first clothing store in town in 1929 at 53

Main Street. Even though the depression began its stranglehold the same year, Silver managed to build his own store in 1930. He expanded in 1966, after the destruction of the Creelman factory. His son Syd Silver (d.1995) was an active member of his community after managing an Orillia store until 1942.

The Dayfoot Boot Factory, one of Georgetown's oldest businesses, was carried on by Harry Dayfoot and his sisters. In 1925 Charles B. Dayfoot returned from Victoria B.C., his base as a traveling salesman, to run the Company. As the Depression took hold, business slowed down for a couple years, but began to improve again about 1934. Charles' son, Arthur Dayfoot

Georgetown Citizen's Band poses outside the old high school. Band is dressed in parade attire and shown with their instruments. The trophy for winning first place at the Toronto Exhibition (CNE) is displayed in front. The photograph was taken September 3, 1931. From left to right: top row: *John Shepherd, Kenneth McDonald, Ray Thompson, Wilfred Gill, Walter Diggins, James Clarke, Thomas Eason, Omar Diggins, Anson Thurston, Roy Magloughlen;* middle row: *Harold Wheeler, Albert Simson, Charlie Willson, Ernest Simson, Kenneth Weston, Joseph Carter, Reuben Eason, Arthur Herbert, Waldo Diggins;* bottom row: *Roy King, Harry Hale, Roy Bradley, John Addy, Ray Norton, A.H.Perrott (Bandmaster), Harvey King, Edward Ballingall, Wilfred Leslie, Mark Clark, Cyril Brandford.* EHS p4

Gordon Alcott,
founder of the
"Little NHL" EHS p8014

Georgetown Post Office opened in 1935 in this fine art-deco building on
a former lumber yard. J.B. Mackenzie and Son were the contractors.
The official opening was postponed due to the death of King George V.

EHS p10434

Two generations of builders,
John B. Mackenzie and
Samuel J. Mackenzie pause for
a portrait in 1931. EHS p8541

decided to become a United Church Minister and a missionary. C.B. Dayfoot, at almost eighty years of age, sold the 100 year old Company effective January 1945.

During the 1920's the knitting machine business of Richard Creelman and his son Clifford began to shrink. The typewriter portion of the company was sold off, and the Company was closed. Richard Creelman died in 1932, ending the family influence in Town.

People found pleasure in their community life during the depression. The arena was busy during the cold seasons and the baseball diamond full during the summer. Movies were popular for a night out, while radio was king at home. The Lorne Scots Band was busy playing at all public affairs and garden parties. In 1935, the Georgetown Pipe Band joined the evening entertainments under pipe major Alex Stewart. In 1938, they merged with the Lorne Scots Pipe Band.

Hockey, always a Georgetown passion, was organized in 1936 for children to enjoy games and competition. Gordon Alcott was the force behind what would become known as the "Little NHL" for about 90 Georgetown boys. The boys were put into teams named after the NHL teams and youngsters used the names of the players in the same big-league positions. The idea spread quickly across the province. A mini-Maple Leafs team, sponsored by the Georgetown Lions Club played against a mini-American team, sponsored by the village of Glen Williams, at Maple Leaf Gardens before a NHL game. One of those boys playing was Weldon "Steamer" Emmerson, later Mayor of Georgetown and ardent supporter of hockey.

The ten years during which Joseph Gibbons served as Mayor from 1933, reflected the quiet years when money was scarce in town. The Toronto Suburban Railway closed in July 1931, the station becoming Irwin Noble's Georgetown Dairy. A community club was formed in 1933 to help the locally unemployed. The auditorium in the Town Hall was opened winter evenings to provide refuge for transients. Federal money was welcome in 1935 when the new post office was erected by J. B. Mackenzie. The motor car was the one pleasure in life for many townsfolk. John and Matthew Armstrong took a gamble, as many people did, and opened a garage on the outskirts of town in 1939. The business is still operating!

The Royal tour of 1939 was a welcome highlight to look forward to. King George VI and Queen Elizabeth were scheduled to stop on the Royal train in Guelph on June 6th. Students from Georgetown went on a special train, with others from Acton and Guelph to Guelph Junction, where they waited for the Royal train to arrive. The train slowed down and the Royal couple waved to everyone from the rear platform. Then it was gone, but students had a better view of the Royal couple than the thousands of locals who waved at the Georgetown train station, as the train thundered through the town.

The 6th September 1939 issue of *The Georgetown Herald* carried the headline "Britain is at War — Canada will play her Part". Brampton was the recruiting site for the Lorne Scots Regiment. In October voluntary registration of women to help in the war effort was carried out at the public library, the United Church and the Barber Greenhouses. Registration was carried out by Misses Sybil Bennett, Mary Lawson, N. Maynard, Isabel Thompson, Mrs. Grieve, Mrs. Dann, Mrs. Carney, Mrs. Barber, Mrs. Coffen, Miss Gillivet and Mrs. Guyot.

There were constant campaigns to raise funds and to support the troops overseas. The Georgetown and District Red Cross, headed by LeRoy Dale, was supplied by the Ashgrove, Georgetown, and Esquesing Women's Institutes, Georgetown High School, the village of Glen Williams, the IODE, Holy Cross Church, Knox Presbyterian Church, St. George's Church, St. John's United Church, Stewarttown Women's Auxilary, Limehouse and Norval Red Cross and the Local Council of Women. The Victory Loan campaign was chaired by William F. Bradley and included door-to door subscriptions and Victory Loan Parades with soldiers, bands and floats.

In April 1940 the Georgetown Soldiers Comforts committee was formed by Mrs. Arthur Reeve, Mrs. Syd MacKenzie, Mrs. Roger Guyot, Mrs. W.V. Grant, Miss Mary Lawson, Mrs. Dan Livingstone, Mrs. Nelson Robinson, Mrs. Arthur Beaumont, and

Mrs. William Mitchell. They sent cigarettes and packages of goods to the boys overseas.

Music was needed during these war years, so in 1942 the Georgetown Girls' Pipe Band was formed. The first shipment of bag pipes was torpedoed by German U-boats and sank to the bottom of the Atlantic Ocean. The McGregor tartan was selected because it was the only material available in sufficient quantities during the war.

Georgetown Boy Scouts and Girl Guides were re-organized in 1943. Mrs. J L. Lambert and Mrs. Anderson led the Guides at St. George's Church. Thirty boys showed up at the Town Hall for Boy Scouts which were organized under Charles Davis and Albert Tost. Jack Armstrong took over as Cubmaster. The Scouts started salvage drives to help with the War effort.

There was more work than workers as record numbers of townspeople served overseas. Prosperous industry makes for a prosperous town. By 1943, the war profits were filtering down through society. The frugal Town Council began to spend their money. The Bank of Montreal (formerly the Merchant's Bank) was forced to close their branch under war regulations so Council purchased the building as a municipal office. A local rationing office opened at the Municipal Offices in 1943 to monitor rationing of items like sugar, tea, coffee, newsprint, butter and gasoline. Due to the strain of the depression, the Arena Company sold out to the Town. Robert Lane was contracted to provide garbage pick up for residents. Night constables during the war included William G. Emmerson, P. J. Fordyce and Mervin Robb.

Georgetown High School delayed the start of school because so many students were involved in war work and in helping on the farms, all of which helped support soldiers overseas. The movie, *Wizard of Oz* came to the Gregory Theatre in January 1940. Angle parking started in downtown Georgetown in September 1939. Walter Biehn became the owner of *The Georgetown Herald* in March 1940. By 1944 Acton, Georgetown and Milton shared a Public Health nurse, Miss Walker, among its schools.

In November 1943 the Georgetown Lumber Mill was gutted by a major fire. The business was started in 1920 when a group of businessmen with Albert Tost and William Kentner took over the lumber business of Henry Pratt Lawson. About 1933, Claude Kentner replaced Mr. Tost as partner and continued the business. They rebuilt the lumber mill and continued in business.

At the end of June 1944, Georgetown was thrilled to hear the voice of Lieutenant Irene "Molly" Mulholland over the radio, speaking from France on an overseas hook-up with the CBC. She was among the first women to reach the beachhead at Normandy with a mobile RCAF hospital. It was the beginning of the end.

On Monday 7 May 1945 news spread that Germany had surrendered. In moments factory whistles, church bells and the fire siren proclaimed the news. As if by magic flags appeared up and down Main Street. The stores, factories and schools emptied as confetti and streamers filled the street. A parade formed at 4:30 and marched to the High School grounds where a service of Thanksgiving was conducted by the Ven.W.G.O. Thompson, Rev. R.C. Todd and Rev. J.E. Ostrom. Evening services were held in churches followed by a street dance, a bonfire at Mill and Market and a burning of Hitler in effigy.

Smith and Stone employees gather for a November portrait outside the factory in 1935.
This is half of a longer photograph. EHS p257

Main Street, Georgetown, Ont

*Looking north on Main Street, about 1949. The Royal Bank sits on the left with the McGibbon Hotel on the right.
Note the interesting street lamps.* EHS p634

Tuesday 8 May 1945 was proclaimed a public holiday by Mayor Harold Cleave. The official announcement was heard on the radio by Prime Minister Winston Churchill followed by President Truman. In the afternoon King George VI and Prime Minister William Lyon Mackenzie King spoke. Services were held Tuesday morning and Holy Cross celebrated Mass on Wednesday morning. A Tuesday evening dance at the Legion culminated the celebrations. The War was over! The boys and girls were coming home.

A grateful Town welcomed veterans home. Employees of Smith and Stone and the Paper Mills were presented with pen and pencil sets, while the villages of Glen Williams, Norval and Limehouse presented watches. Although the Town hoped to raise funds to issue each Town veteran with a $50 Canada Savings Bond, the response allowed only a $20 cheque, presented at Dominion Day ceremonies by Mayor Joseph Gibbons on 1 July 1947. The Legion was renovated for its influx of new members. A new memorial tablet and a tablet at the Memorial Arena were dedicated in September 1948.

The return of so many men and women to Georgetown resulted in an acute housing shortage. Two surveys of Victory housing were opened up to help relieve the housing shortage by 1948. Churchill Crescent and Normandy Boulevard joined the streetscape of the Town. The long abandoned Barber estate, Berwick Hall, was turned into apartments by Bill Bradley in 1948.

The prosperous war years were reflected in the new attitude of Town Council towards providing services for its citizens. The changes were fast and furious. The "village constable" became a relict of the past in 1947 when the Town decided to contract their policing to the Ontario Provincial Police. In 1946, the Town hired a recreational director. The Town Hall auditorium was renovated and teen dances, known locally as "swing and sway" sessions, were sponsored Friday nights. The Town purchased a truck to do their own snowplowing in 1947. In 1948, garbage was picked up twice weekly, and the arena got an artificial ice making machine! A decision to sell the municipal offices to the Royal Bank resulted in the enlargement of the 1925 waterworks building to serve as the new municipal and police office. The Town was also forced to replace their water supply system at a cost of $80,000. In 1949 they took over the sewage disposal plant begun two years earlier.

While the machinery of government grew, post-war industry was suffering. In 1947, the Dayfoot Shoe factory closed its doors. Ontario Hydro was running short of power, causing blackouts and forcing industries in town to alternately close down one extra day of the week. On November 15, 1948 the Provincial Paper Mill closed the "lower mill", the original Barber Paper Mill, affecting 80 employees. Joseph McMenemy was the last superintendent of the enterprise begun by the Barber brothers 94 years previously. It was a bleak Christmas in Georgetown.

Georgetown hosts the Orange Parade on 12 July 1961. Concrete pipes indicate preparations for sewer work. EHS p238

CHAPTER EIGHT

The Baby Boom

The decade of the 1950s witnessed the transformation of Georgetown in a way not seen since the arrival of the railway one hundred years earlier. This decade marked the end of small towns operating in isolation as southern Ontario became urbanized. Industries became owned by large corporations without local family connections.

The decade began ominously. The April 1st 1950 editorial in *The Herald* was entitled 'A Growing Town Has Difficulties" Editor Biehn listed the issues facing Council that year — new schools, sewer extensions, improvements to water supply, hydro supply, new roads and sidewalks… and concluded they cannot be delayed. Georgetown was facing major expenditures.

The 1951 census revealed a population of 3 452 persons. Waves of European immigrants were swelling the size of Toronto — an entire community called Rexdale was being built on Etobicoke farmland. The baby boom was swelling Georgetown Public School. In 1952, a second public school opened, named in honour of Howard Wrigglesworth, a former principal who had died suddenly. The new school opened under Principal William Kinrade. Georgetown joined the North Halton District High School Board. The Town built a new fire hall, after Bell Telephone gave notice they would no longer sound the fire alarm, because Georgetown would have dial tele-

phones in 1953. The spread of Town beyond the traditional boundaries was obvious to Gladys Caldwell, who opened the IGA supermarket on Guelph Street across from the Dominion Seed House gardens. Al Norton led a campaign to have a Liquor Control Board store opened in Georgetown and was successful. It opened in the part of the Legion building.

The growing population gave Ken Langdon, a local lawyer and magistrate, the idea of reviving the golf course closed by John Willoughby in 1940. Only sheep grazed where natty golfers once putted. Langdon gathered 15 interested men to form the North Halton Golf and Country Club. They issued shares and on 1 April 1954 the new company purchased the land from John Willoughby. The Club expanded to eighteen holes in 1969.

The swelling population demanded facilities, but the shrinking industrial base meant higher property taxes. In 1954, the Town taxes were 58% residential, 23.5% industrial, and the rest was farm or small buildings. The solution to Georgetown's problems walked into the Municipal offices. Rex Heslop, builder of Rexdale, proposed a massive housing development between Georgetown and Norval. Although the Town would need to build a sewage disposal plant and provide other services, Heslop guaranteed them his survey would yield a 60% residential and

Natural gas begins to flow in Georgetown in 1956. Shown left to right are Mary Biehn, Delma Heslop, Walter Gray (rear), John D. Kelly, Mrs. Ruth Allen, Len Ward (rear), Edna & Mayor John T. Armstrong and Reeve Stan Allen. EHS p382

40% industrial tax base. It was music to the ears of Georgetown Council. The deal was struck between Heslop and Council under Mayor Jack Armstrong.

Construction began in January 1955, creating some immediate benefits. Varian Industries was attracted to Town. The construction garnered Georgetown a natural gas hook-up. Gas began to flow in August 1956.

The Town budget continued to be stretched to cover an ever widening range of services. Foremost was the need for a police department. The Provincial government ordered all towns over 2000 souls to police themselves. Roy Haley began his 12 year career as Police Chief on June 1, 1955. A new hydro office was constructed beside the post office. McClure Funeral Home decided to give up the ambulance business in 1956. The Town purchased the ambulance and a volunteer brigade was organized the following year.

The new subdivision brought with it children — lots of children. Educational facilities were the first priority. February 1957 marked the opening of Harrison School, Georgetown's third. Park School and Holy Cross Roman Catholic Separate Schools opened in 1958. George Kennedy School followed the next year. Georgetown High School had a west wing added in 1954 and east wing in 1958. In 1959, the venerable original building was swept away and a modern building replaced it the following year. When school let out for the summer, the children wanted a place

In July 1955, these members of the Georgetown Women's Institute visited the Beatty Bros. Limited plant in Fergus to view the very latest in washday equipment. Photograph courtesy Annie Livingstone.

The simple lines of the new addition to the Georgetown High School contrast with the imposing 1889 structure in this 1958 photograph.
EHS p13465

Mayor Jack Armstrong
has his photo taken with
Councillor Anne Currie on
inauguration night, 1960.

Photograph courtesy Anne Currie.

*Mayor Jack Armstrong and
Rex Heslop point out a sign
advertising a new house model
available at reasonable cost
in the Delrex subdivision
about 1959.* EHS p8801

The last steam train in regular use passed through Georgetown in 1959. This winter visitor attracted a crowd in February 1965.

EHS p8107

to swim. The local Lions Club, founded here in 1931, spearheaded a campaign to build an outdoor pool behind the arena. The cool waters were first enjoyed in August 1956.

The Town was obviously in need of tax dollars. The promised industrial base was not materializing. After negotiating with Delrex Developments, it became obvious that they were unable to meet their contractual agreement. The citizens urged Council to take drastic action to get industry into Town, rather than leave it in the hands of the developer. In August 1959, the Town Council amended the contract with Delrex to allow cash payments per lot in lieu of maintaining the 40% industrial / commercial ratio.

The final year of the decade really pushed Georgetown into the modern era! The unexpected closure of the AVRO Arrow project by the Federal government on 20 February 1959, put over 600 Georgetown people out of work. Accordingly, in April, the Town was forced to raise taxes substantially.

On 20 April 1959, the last regular steam train passed through Georgetown. This transportation milestone was matched later in the year when the Highway 401 overpass at Highway 25 opened which was immediately followed by Halton OPP being called to investigate their first accident on the superhighway!

*Barry James and
Danny Clark
face off in 1965.*
EHS p8088

*Georgetown Figure Skating Club
instructor Marilyn Barber poses with
Sharon Hewitt, Linda Mooney,
Laurie Hyde, Julie Smart,
Janet Mooney, Robin Alcorn and
Nancy Hall. The photo appeared
in the* Georgetown Herald
in February 1965. EHS p8098

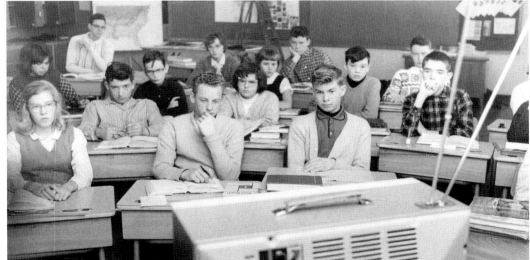

*Television becomes an
educational tool at
Park School in 1966.*
EHS p8711

Georgetown and District Hospital was opened in June 1961. This aerial photograph from that time reveals the size of the original structure when compared with today's facility. EHS p13702

Striking workers at Smith and Stone block a train from unloading its freight in May 1964.
EHS p208

The Avian Aircraft gyroplane was being tested in 1963. The Georgetown company started production in 1966 of the 2/180 model at a cost of $17,500. EHS p249

Georgetown Air Rangers celebrate international night with Carol Lane, Linda Emery, Diane Carr, Arlene Edge, Sharon MacArthur, Mrs. P.J. Bundy, Susan Asseltine and Christine McIntyre in April 1965. EHS p8189

Wolf Cubs learn their knots about 1965. EHS p8799

In May, Governor-General Vincent Massey visited town for about 30 minutes. He was greeted by Mayor Armstrong and dignitaries at the station with a Lorne Scots honour guard while Alf Perrott conducted the Citizen's Band in "The Maple Leaf Forever". All the school children assembled to meet him as well as Scouts and Guides in uniform. He laid a wreath at the cenotaph and returned to the train.

Everyday life changed as well in 1959. Irwin Noble took his last milk run with horse and wagon. Delrex Plaza opened on Highway Seven to serve the residents of east Georgetown. Letter carrier service was inaugurated which led to the establishment of a newspaper boy to deliver *The Herald*.

Fortunately, industry did locate here in 1959. Avian Aircraft was opened by five former AVRO engineers to develop a vertical take-off gyroplane. Standard Products opened to manufacture car parts, providing much needed employment for many people. The government offered a "Winter Works" programme to aid the unemployed.

L'Eglise Sacré-Coeur on Guelph Street was built in 1885 as Holy Cross Church.
It was rededicated in 1966 and has served the French Catholics of Georgetown since then. EHS p10628b

The population reached 10,000 souls in 1960 and a long, successful campaign to build a Georgetown Hospital reached fruition. Years of traveling to Guelph Hospital by Doctors Chamberlain, Williams, MacIntosh, McAllister, Paul and Thompson were finally ended. The Georgetown Hospital Association was founded in 1956 under the leadership of Jack Gunn. They sponsored Victoria Day celebrations at Fairgrounds Park and netted $380 for the new hospital. From those small beginnings began a four year effort to gain government support and a door-to-door campaign to raise local funds. On 12 June 1960, the sod turning took place and work began, culminating in the official opening on 17 June 1961. The first baby born at Georgetown and District Memorial Hospital was Ron Marchand, followed by Christine Moore on 28 June 1961.

Other changes about Town included the removal of the cenotaph to Remembrance Park in September 1960. This was the first of several small Town parks. In the original Fairgrounds Park, the grandstand burned to the ground in August 1968. The first 'nightclub' opened as the Riviera on January 1, 1962 in Norval. The YMCA was organized here the same year. A larger post office opened in 1963 at Maple and Guelph Streets. The United Church Girl's School at Cedar Vale closed in 1963, and was transformed into a park and community centre in 1966 as the Town's Centennial project. Cable television became available to residents in 1967. In Canada's Centennial Year, the population had reached 15 465!

Local churches were packed for Easter 1962 as this photograph of worshippers leaving St. John's United Church attests. EHS p8662

Georgetown Girls' Pipe Band members pose on the steps of Parliament Hill in 1966.

Photograph courtesy Dovie Fiebig.

Georgetown now had diversity in its population which it had never had in the past. In religion, congregations grew. The Baptists added a Maple Avenue and a Mountainview Road Church in 1960. The old Main Street Chapel closed in 1970, becoming the first home of the Christian and Missionary Alliance Church in 1974. This Church was founded on 2 October 1966 at Cedarvale Park with Pastor Paul Collins and four members! St. Andrew's became the second United Church in Town. The Lutheran Church was organized here in 1963. The Re-Organized Church of Latter Day Saints and Jehovah's Witnesses opened. The Pentecostal Church came in 1971, building their new Pentecostal Assembly building on Highway Seven in 1974. The Dutch Christian Reformed Church, was organized here in 1957, meeting in the Stewarttown Hall until the former Radial Railway station and dairy was renovated to their purpose. They met at the Main Street location until 1966 when they built their own church on Trafalgar Road. It was dedicated on 10 February 1967.

The Roman Catholics, a tiny mission of the Acton Church since 1883, became a parish in 1956. They built a school in 1958, establishing the Separate School Board. In 1960, Father Otger Devent, with the 350 families, started planning the erection of a large new church beside Silver Creek. The new Holy Cross opened on 14 March 1965.

The vacant 1885 Holy Cross Church was rededicated on 26 June 1966 as L'Eglise Sacré Coeur. About 150 French-speaking Catholic families created their own parish. While this area has no history of a concentration of French-Canadians, the process was achieved in a very short time. In 1947, Father Clovis Beauregard and his niece, Therese St. Jean moved their orphan boys farm from St. Catharines, to Georgetown. The twenty Acadian boys learned apple farming and decided to remain here in adulthood. To assist in the seasonal apple business other Acadian families moved here and the process began to snowball. By 1957, a French-Canadian Association was formed, with Miss St. Jean as its leader.

Holy Cross School recognized the growing French fact in 1960 with the introduction of bilingual classes. The Association kept pressure on the Board to provide more services. In 1965, a bilingual kindergarten was established in the basement of a restaurant while the Ministry of Education, L'Association Canadienne Française, and the Georgetown Separate School Board volleyed the *fait-accompli* back and forth. On May 10, some parents boycotted the school, and on 17 May, they marched to the building and staged a sit-in. Supporters from Galt and Alabama arrived. Reverend Father Devent became involved followed by anonymous bomb threats, which involved the police and fire marshal. The sit-in was called off and bilingual kindergarten was introduced on Wednesday May 19. When the County Boards of Education were established on 1 January 1969, L'école Sacré Coeur achieved distinct status within the Holy Cross building.

The Christian Reformed congregation realized their dream of a separate school when they opened Georgetown Christian School on Trafalgar Road, in September 1965 with 81 students under principal George Petrusma. Mr. Petrusma ran the school until June 1989. Marianne Vangoor is the current principal.

Another housing development, Moore Park, was carried out

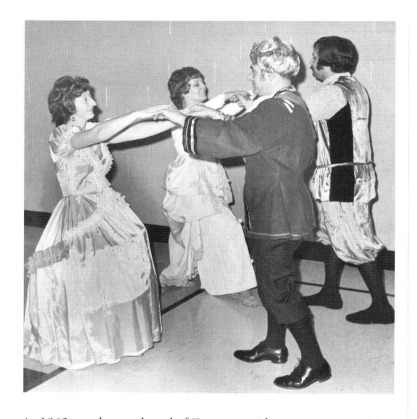

*Gord and Cathy Hunt support Pioneer Days
on Main Street in 1967.* Photo courtesy Dovie Fiebig.

*Georgetown Little Theatre dancers practice for their
production of* Cinderella. *Shown in the 1971 photo are
Derek and Pat Jones, John Hopkins and Diane Barber.* EHS p8733

in 1962, on the north end of Town, providing some competition for the Heslop development. Relations between the Rex Heslop and the Town continued to deteriorate. In an effort to win public understanding, Heslop backed the creation of a new newspaper in 1961, *The Georgetown Leader.* There was certainly plenty to report! On the 26 October, 1961, Rex Heslop was arrested and charged with attempting to bribe Mayor Ernest Hyde. The

Mayor had tape recorded telephone conversations with Heslop which were used as evidence. Rex Heslop was found guilty on 6 June 1962 and sentenced to one month in jail. Ironically, Council passed a bylaw that same month which released the developer from his 1954 agreement to provide a 60/40 tax base. *The Leader* folded at the end of the year and by the spring of 1964, Heslop had sold his interests in the Delrex subdivision.

The Delrex decade had irrevocably altered the face of Georgetown. While the large industrial base was never achieved, industry did drift to Town. Some stayed a short time while others are still in operation. ArtCast (1964), Economy Forms (1964), Die Mold Tool (1964), Georgetown Book Warehouse (1965), Fortamix (1968), Curwood Packaging (1969), Irwin–Dorsey Ltd. (1969), Gage Stationery (1970), Labelmasters (1971), KNR Concrete Products (1973), Neilson's (1974), United Fire Safety (1975), and Rockwell (1977) are all examples of new industries. Big corporate names like Zellers (1971) and McDonald's (1975) were added to the business roster.

Nevertheless, expanded government services and political in-fighting at all levels, continued to plague the Town. In June 1966, the Town constructed the new landmark of Georgetown — the water tank on Todd Road. It stood 1000 feet above sea level and enabled the Town pumps to remain off until the water level dropped in the tank to the point where the pumps were sent a signal to start up again. The cost of the police force rose. By 1969, the force under Harvey Lowe had reached 17 men. The school facilities were completed with Stewarttown in

Georgetown postmaster Harold Marshall is presented with congratulations on his retirement from the Prime Minister of Canada by J. O'Connell in November 1973 at the Georgetown Legion. EHS p16373

1966, Centennial in 1966, Joseph Gibbons in 1970, and St. Francis of Assisi in 1971. But now escalating salaries for teachers, police constables and town employees played havoc with taxes. The Town again was in need of a sewage plant expansion by 1971.

The solution, as planned by the provincial government, was regional government. In effect, only one government for the entire township was to exist, with responsibility for services clearly divided between the municipality, the region, and the province. Consequently, on 1 January 1974, the Corporation of the Town of Georgetown ceased to exist. The Corporation of the Town of Halton Hills took on the responsibilities of the Acton, Georgetown, and Esquesing Councils, under Mayor Tom Hill, former Esquesing Reeve.

The prosperity which the Village of Georgetown dreamed of in 1865, when it became a Village, was the very reason why the Province ended 109 years of autonomy. Regional government also lumped Georgetown together with Esquesing, its favourite Council to squabble with and with Acton, long-time rival for industry, hockey, lacrosse and baseball! Prospects did not look promising.

The Lorne Scots pipe band welcomes a Credit Valley steam engine to Georgetown station for the inaugural run of the GO train in April 1974. EHS p16379

CHAPTER NINE

Regional Government

The abolition of Georgetown Town Council was regretted by most. However, numerous jurisdictional problems and growing financial burdens placed on municipalities, convinced politicians to make the best of it. A new Town Council was elected in 1974 with Glen Williams resident Thomas J. Hill as Mayor. The new Council met in the Esquesing offices built in 1963 on Trafalgar Road. Town employees worked in several buildings throughout the three former corporations.

The new Corporation presided over a Town with an improving economy. Marywood Meadows, built houses near the hospital and townhouse building on Maple Avenue provided housing while industry prospered and expanded their facilities. A new transit system, dubbed the GO Train started service in 1974 with Georgetown station as the terminus. While the Town budget was in poor shape, the new Council approved a new arena and indoor swimming pool at the High School. Both opened in 1975. In the same spirit of an expanding local economy, councillors planned a large municipal complex to house the fragmented bureaucracy. Over 2500 residents signed a petition against the idea, which Council dropped in February 1977.

Georgetown was shocked that same month to see Domtar close its doors, putting 176 out of work. The second of Georgetown's three paper mills was finished. Domtar started in 1910 as Georgetown Coated Paper.

The *Georgetown Independent* was launched on 17 October 1973 by the Dills family of Acton to compete with the *Georgetown Herald,* which in turn became the *Halton Hills Herald* and began covering Acton news.

The *Georgetown Herald* was sold in 1973 by Walter and Mary Biehn after years of making it an informative community newspaper. Mary (d. 1976) wrote about local events in her column, "Chatting". Walter Biehn (1915–2005) purchased the paper in 1940 and kept in touch with local news by becoming a Town Councillor, belonging to the Lion's Club, supporting the Chamber of Commerce, being Chairman of the Georgetown Board of Education and a member of the YMCA board.

The *Independent* was edited by Hartley Coles from its founding until 1991. The two papers shared the profitable decades of the seventies and eighties.

Retail businesses and services grew tremendously for the next dozen years while industry and housing remained fairly stable. From a population of 17 582 in 1974, only 193 people were added to the Town population a full dozen years later. Costs rose but taxpayers did not. Vacant parcels of land in town were slowly developed as first taxes and then land values shot up.

The grand old lady of Georgetown education, Chapel Street School closed in 1974, and fell to the wreckers ball in 1980. Shrinking school populations also closed Howard Wrigglesworth School in 1986. The old building housed L'Ecole Sacré-Coeur, Holy Cross East Campus, St. Francis of Assisi for a year while they renovated, a Brampton High School grade nine class, the Ontario Early Learning Centre and the Gary Allan High School opened in 2004 for students having difficulty with the regular system.

The grand old lady of Georgetown education, Chapel Street School, is shown here about 1977, when it closed its doors. Her uncertain future dominated local discussions until demolition in 1980. EHS p542

Speyside School, also closed in 1986, was the first home to the new Bishop Reding Catholic High School. Many Georgetown and Acton students attended the school until the new High School on Main Street, Milton opened in 1988.

The old Congregational Church received a new lease on life in 1981, when an expanded library, an art gallery and the 267 seat John Elliott Theatre were added. The former church sanctuary became an art gallery, giving Georgetown and area artists their first public venue. The theatre was named for local businessman, politician and community supporter, John Alwyn Elliott. It has become the home of the Little Theatre group and the Globe Productions.

The Bennett Health Care Centre was built for Georgetown's aging population in 1985, adjoining the hospital. A large addition in 1999 changed the facility to a long-term care facility. It was officially opened by Mayor Marilyn Serjeantson, Centre director Connell Smith and Ted Chudleigh, MPP.

The old funeral home on Edith Street was given up in favour of a new facility on Trafalgar Road in 1986. J. S. "Jim" Jones, who had taken over the direction of the McClure Funeral Home in 1954, moved the business to the new facility and retired in 1989. The business is run today by Phil Jones, Marg Jones and Toby Chisholm.

The Esquesing Historical Society was formed in January 1975, as a reaction to the merging of the three former corporations into Halton Hills. The first president was John McDonald. The Society has raised awareness about local history by collecting, preserving and sharing their knowledge.

Top Georgetown Employers of 1986

Company	Contact	Employees
Varian Canada Inc.	Joe Calderelli	356
Smith and Stone (1982) Inc.	S. Tooke	286
Neilson Ltd.	J. Wilson	275
Standard Products (Canada) Ltd.	U.B. Fieback	194
Cercor Inc.	Barry Hadley	150
Curwood Packaging Ltd.	B.H. Kedwell	130
Rockwell International of Canada	Mike Pascoe	100
P. G. Bell	A. Buisman or G. N. Tolhurst	89
Watch Tower Bible and Tract Society	Kenneth Little	86
Georgetown Terminal Warehouses Ltd.	Brenda Sisnett	75
Baltimore Aircoil of Canada	R.J. Hampton	70
Ferro Structural Steel Ltd.	J. Salamon	63
Provincial Papers	F.C. Aggiss	62

Maple Avenue Baptist Church was built in 1960.
This photograph from 1974 shows the structure before
reconstruction of the sanctuary in 2000. EHS p16357

The former Congregational Church at Church and Market Street
has served as the library from 1895. In 1981 an addition
expanded the library along Market Street, freeing the former
sanctuary for use as an art gallery. EHS p12082

They helped form Heritage Halton Hills in 1986, which designates historical buildings in the Town.

Residents continued to enjoy regular events like the Little Theatre, formed in 1960, and the Globe Theatre. The Chamber of Commerce sponsored the first Business in Georgetown show in 1984 and the Town Recreation department biannually hosts a Sports and Leisure show. The Highland Games, Optimist Bang-a-Rama, and the Fall Fair return every year.

The closing years of the decade saw Georgetown enjoying a boom, along with the province. In 1985, A&P received a large expansion and face-lift. Building of the massive "Georgetown South" began in 1989. Bell Canada acknowledged the growth in their business in 1986 when the Georgetown exchange of 877 doubled in size with the addition of 873. The impact of Georgetown South development resulted in the addition of the 702 exchange in 1993. Since the popularity of cellar telephones, residents are now used to any prefix to reach a friend in Georgetown.

More than ten years after citizens rose up in anger at the prospect of a town hall for Halton Hills, politicians once more began a campaign to unite Civic employees into one facility. This time the opponents were drowned out by almost $50 000 in donations of gifts and cash by residents.

The Dog and Suds Drive-In on Guelph Street offered hamburgers, hot dogs and shakes on Highway Seven. McDonald's Restaurant and Prosperity One now occupy the site. EHS p16365

Mayor Russell Miller casts his vote on the Charlottetown Accord in 1992. Elections Canada officers Malcolm MacLeod and Fraser Robin look on. Halton Hills This Week, 28 October 1992

The blue box programme began the same year, as environmental concerns became prevalent. The unveiling of a plan to put garbage in an Acton quarry in 1987, spawned the birth of POWER and aligned Georgetown citizens, activists, and politicians on the same side of the fence to oppose it.

The new decade put the brakes on the economy with a recession in 1991. The great housing boom in Georgetown South ground to a halt, the Town had to readjust their budget and business was poor. On 31 March 1991, the final chapter in Georgetown's paper history was written. The Provincial Papers closed its doors forever. This building was built to house Barber's Coated Paper Mill in 1905. Smith and Stone, electrical manufacturers, had difficulties in the 1980s and suffered a strike. The recession in 1991 exacerbated the situation and finally in September 1992, closure was announced after more than 70 years in the Town.

Regional government brought big government to Georgetown. Regional government also brought improved services and better facilities to the residents of the Town. The twenty years since the creation of Halton Hills saw industry continue to shrink and Georgetown changed from a typical Ontario small town to a large suburb with a small town feel. As a new Georgetown grew south of the river valley, Brampton grew closer and closer. Georgetown had entered into the orbit of the Greater Toronto Region!

The Town of Halton Hills opened their multi-million dollar Civic Centre on 26 August 1989. The following year Halton Hills Hydro opened an expanded headquarters in Acton, closing the Georgetown office on Mill Street.

Mackenzie Lumber building on James Street was built by Henry Pratt Lawson in 1897.
It has been renovated into commercial spaces. EHS p10745

Victory in Europe day is the opportunity to light a candle at the Georgetown cenotaph and to personally thank a veteran. Veterans pose on 7 May 2004 with students from Holy Cross, St. Francis of Assisi, St. Catherine of Alexandria, Christ the King and St. Brigid Catholic Schools. Photograph courtesy J. M. Rowe.

CHAPTER TEN

Georgetown's Growth Continues

Georgetown East was the moniker used to apply to the Delrex developments of the 1950s and 1960s. It was sometimes used to differentiate the "old" Town from the newcomers.

Once again a geographical label has been used to differentiate one section of town from another. Sometimes, the label is used in a negative way, but unlike the Delrex development which did drain the vitality from the downtown, the new "town" south of the ravine, has only infused vitality into the existing Town.

Georgetown "South" was begun in 1989 and except for a 1991 recession has continued unabated. As this book goes to press in early 2006, the building continues. Unlike "Delrex" the development of this land was undertaken by several builders and so "Georgetown South" became the all-encompassing term readily applied by residents north and south of the ravine. École Sacré-Coeur was the first new school to open on Miller Drive in 1994, followed by St. Brigid Catholic School further down the street, in 1996. Long-time Holy Cross teacher, Cynthia Tobin was the first principal of the large school. The explosive growth of St. Brigid led to the opening of St. Catherine of Alexandria Catholic School on Barber Drive, also opened under Cynthia Tobin. The Public School Board opened their first school in 2004 on Eaton Drive, backing onto the Park shared by St. Brigid School. Silver Creek Public School opened under Principal Wendy Harrison with 784 students!

Halton Catholic District School Board trustee Irene McCauley, who marked 25 years as a trustee in 2005, worked diligently to get these schools for Georgetown. Her work culminated in the opening of Christ the King Catholic Secondary School on Guelph Street in September 2002 with transfers from Bishop Reding Catholic High School in Milton and new local students, under Principal Nijole Vaitonis. It opened with 640 students.

The growth in business was slow at first, but before long, downtown Georgetown stores filled up. While the McGibbon Hotel still dominates the street, several landmark businesses have gone. In December 2000, Goodlet's, a hardware store since 1879 closed its doors. The store run by Doug, Doris, Jim and Barb Goodlet has now become The Shepherd's Crook, a British Pub owned by Rick Ruggle. In June 2005, Henry Helfant of H&H Clothing closed the doors on 54 years of business.

Fine dining in Georgetown has never offered such a variety of choice — The Cellar, Simply Bleu, 77 Market Street, Main Street Inn, Mattina's Cucina and even YoYo's, a Japanese restau-

Mayor Marilyn Serjeantson, Moya Johnson, Rev. Gerald Rennie, and Ted Drewlo of Halton Hills stand by truck showing new Halton Hills logo in August 1997. The pillars represent the strength of the business and industrial community and the wavy lines represent the two rivers within Halton Hills. EHS p15981

The strip plazas on Highway #7 are busy and the Georgetown Marketplace Mall is often crowded. One busy landmark is the Georgeview Restaurant, built about 1954. It was taken over in 1967 by Poppy and John Cambouris with Irene and Bill Leou. They continue to operate the business today. Another landmark, Georgetown Fruit Market, closed its doors in 2005, with the retirement of Joe and Maria Scibilia. They opened their first market in Georgetown in 1972 with partner Franco Cuzzupe.

The 1959 Loblaws underwent a large expansion in June 1998. One of the features of the new place was a mural of local scenes painted by Barb Symons, resident of Lakeshore area of Toronto. In January 1999, the Georgetown IGA was gutted by fire after three arsonists set the landmark 1954 store ablaze. It was managed by Patrick Begin and owned by his family. One firefighter, Bruce Morrison suffered a broken leg, while two other firefighters were injured.

Since that time the IGA brand has gone and Sobey's has had its eye on Georgetown. They built a large "Price Chopper" store in the vacant land between Boston Pizza and Home Hardware, on Guelph Street, in 2006. In the meantime, Loblaws is pursuing aggressive expansion with a whole new complex on the Dominion Seed House lands, between McDonald's and Christ the King Secondary School. The new one-stop shopping Super

rant, which replaced the one-time famous Spot-on-Seven. The swank Riviera Club, which opened on the banks of the Credit River in 1962, leads a new life as Nashville North, a name which proclaims western line dancing, but hides the hip hop nights!

Centre opened in 2006. A&P is also planning a large new store to serve Georgetown South at Mountainview and Argyll Roads.

After bringing prosperity to Georgetown businesses, the residents of Georgetown South received their own plaza in the spring of 2001 at the corner of Mountainview and Argyll. The new facility was anchored by a 7-Eleven store and gas bar and a Shopper's Drug Mart. Pharmacist Alex Bertrand opened the new store in October 2001.

As a millennium project, a Georgetown Committee was established to refurbish Remembrance Park at James and Charles Streets. After appealing to the people of town, they received 445 donations. Chairman Martin Boomsma felt the Park turned out even better than he expected. It was officially re-dedicated in October 2000.

The newly refurbished Remembrance Park was the site of a visit on 21 October 2001 of HRH The Duke of Kent, Colonel-in-Chief of the Lorne Scots Regiment. He was here to celebrate the 135th anniversary of the Regiment. HRH was greeted by Mayor Kathy Gastle, Regional Chair Joyce Savoline and MP Julian Reed. He lay at wreath at the cenotaph and was presented with a basket of Canadiana by students of Park School.

The birthplace of the "Little NHL" was suffering from a lack of hockey facilities, due to the population growth. In 2001,

The Lorne Scots parade at the newly re-dedicated Remembrance Park in October 2001. EHS p11994

work finally began on twinning the ice pads at Gordon Alcott Arena. The project received a boost and a new name in April 2001 when Moldmasters, Georgetown's largest employer, donated a considerable sum to the project. The company, which came to Georgetown in the 1970s, was started in 1963 by Jobst and Waltraud Gellert.

The Rotary Club presents a phonic ear to John Elliot Theatre manager Cecil Peacock (far right). The presentation was made in November 1997 by Al Fraser, Dave Stevenson and Bob Walterson. EHS p15944

The Gellert Centre was officially opened on 13 June 2004 by Mayor Rick Bonnette at a ceremony which included athlete Donovan Bailey and the provincial finance minister. The new facility in Georgetown South boasts a lap pool, leisure pool, sauna, hot tub and meeting room.

New soccer fields opened on the Devereaux farm at Maple and Trafalgar Road, after the Town acquired the property. A local group headed by Anne Lawlor, is working to restore the historic farmhouse for Town use. A six acre woodlot was established as the Jubilee Woodlot in 2003, after a suggestion by Matthew Rowe of Glen Williams to honour the Golden Jubilee of Queen Elizabeth II.

Smaller housing developments have also filled in spaces within the Town. More townhouses were built on River Drive, while the Mushroom Factory property on Mountainview Road has slowly developed. A triangle of land was developed as Trafalgar Country between the two rail lines and linked to Princess Anne Drive through the CNR underpass which originally served the Toronto Suburban railway.

Georgetown has had four great periods of growth and prosperity. The first was the arrival of the Barber Brothers in 1837. The second was the arrival of the railway in 1856. The third boom took place about 100 years later — 1956, with the development of Delrex subdivision. The fourth period of prosperity has been the development of Georgetown South. This is a period of growth which continues as this book goes to press. The long-term effects are not yet history, but the growth of Town continues for the long term! The new residents praise the small town atmosphere of Georgetown, while the long-time residents recall the quiet town of their childhood. As Georgetown residents reflect on the future of their small town, uncertainty looms. Only time will provide an answer.

Queen's Golden Jubilee medal recipients gather with Mayor Kathy Gastle and Regional Chair Joyce Savoline to open the Jubilee Woodlot behind St. Catherine of Alexandria School on 6 July 2003. Photograph courtesy J.M. Rowe.

POLITICAL LEADERS OF GEORGETOWN

ESQUESING WARDENS

1821	Charles Kennedy & John Stewart
1822	Peter McCallum & Wm. Kent
1823	Peter McCallum & Thomas Stephens
1824	Thomas Barbour & Wm. Kent
1825	Thomas Barbour & Thomas Fyfe
1826	David Darling & Christian Barnes
1828	James Hume & John Boomer
1829	Samuel Kennedy & Alex McNab
1830	Donald McKinnon & Ezra Adams
1831	John Menzies & Morris Kennedy
1832	Donald McKinnon & Malcom McNaughton
1833	James Hume & Thomas Fyfe
1834	Thomas Fyfe & John Burns
1835	Benajah Williams & Thomas Barbour
1836	James Fraser & James Skirrows
1837	Charles Kennedy, James Skirrows & John McNaughton
1838	John Burns, Edward Leonard & James Stark
1839	Francis Huston, Robert Shortreed & Samuel Kennedy
1840	Charles Kennedy, Joseph Standish & Finlay McNaughton
1841	John Stewart, John Stull & John Menzies

DISTRICT COUNCILLORS

1842	Charles Kennedy & Finlay McNaughton
1843	William Barber
1844	Ninian Lindsay
1845–1846	William Barber
1847–1848	William Clay
1849	John McNaughton

ESQUESING REEVES

1850	John McNaughton
1851–1856	James Young
1857–1858	John McNaughton
1859	William Barber
1860–1866	William Clay

GEORGETOWN REEVES

1865	James Young
1866	Francis Barclay
1867–1876	John R. Barber
1877–1878	David McKenzie
1879–1881	William McLeod
1882	John R. Barber

GEORGETOWN REEVES *continued*

1883–1888	William McLeod
1889	William Freeman
1890–1892	George H. Kennedy
1893	David McKenzie
1894–1896	Joseph Barber
1897–1898	W. H. Kahrs
1899	W.H. Kennedy
1900	F. J. Barber
1901–1902	Dr. Nixon
1903–1904	R. D. Warren
1905–1907	John Willoughby
1908–1909	John G. Harley
1910	Edward McCannah
1911	Lachlan Grant
1912–1913	Joseph M. Moore
1914–1916	L. E. Fleck
1917–1918	Herbert Heartwell
1919	Lachlan Grant
1920–1921	LeRoy Dale

MAYORS OF GEORGETOWN

1922–1926	LeRoy Dale
1927	Donald McIntyre
1928–1929	LeRoy Dale
1930–1933	J. B. Mackenzie
1934–1943	Joseph Gibbons
1944–1946	Harold Cleave
1947–1949	Joseph Gibbons
1950–1951	Harold Cleave
1952–1959	John Armstrong
1960–1961	Ernest T. Hyde
1962	Douglas Sargent
1963	Ernest T. Hyde
1964–1968	Joseph Gibbons
1969–1970	Wheldon Emmerson
1971–1973	William R. Smith

MAYORS OF HALTON HILLS

1974–1978	Thomas J. Hill
1979–1983	Peter Pomeroy
1983–1993	Russell T. Miller
1994–2000	Marilyn Sarjeantson
2001–2003	Kathy Gastle
2003–	Rick Bonnette

LEST WE FORGET

WORLD WAR I
Flight Lieutenant C. Barber
Flight Lieutenant C. Somerville
Lieutenant E. Leslie
Sergeant James Blair
Sergeant W.C. Granger
Sergeant Obs. H. Nelle
Sergeant J. Moore
Lance Corporal A.S. Mino
Private J. Campbell
Private J. Cowan
Private H. Francis
Private S. Godfrey
Private J. Presswood
Private I. Green
Private H. Hickey
Private P. King
Private W. King
Private J.E. Kennedy
Private W. Loud
Private D. McKenzie
Private G. Mason
Private W. Phillips
Private G.H. Sleightholme

Private G. H. Spires
Private S. Stawicky
Private E. Cornish

WORLD WAR II
Flying Officer John Evans
Flying Officer William McLaughlin
Flying Officer Norman Bailey
Lieutenant Bruce Zimmerman
Pilot Officer Carman Sutcliff
Pilot Officer James Louth
Flying Officer William Murphy
Flying Sergeant Lawrence Beaumont
Sergeant Stewart Maclaren
Sergeant Hubert F. Tost
Corporal Hedley Shaw
Leading Aircraftsman William Carney
Corporal Carl Hyde
Rifleman J. Davis
Private Harry Dickenson
Private Stanley Dickenson
Private Claude Dillon
Private Edward Doyle
Private Ervine Hilts

Private Fred Kidd
Private John O'Kane
Private John Oliver
Private H. Simpson
Private William Wylie
Private Robert Wylie
Private Jack Kendall
Private Reg Blair
Private John Hemphill
Private George Latimer
Private Harvey Davidson
Private J. Jamieson
Private William Kay
Private Clarence Beaumont
A/B Victor Millar
Driver R. Allen
Trooper Howard Conn

KOREAN CONFLICT
Corporal Ron Edmunds
Private Ken Norton

UNITED NATIONS SERVICE
Private Chris Dodge

APPENDIX III

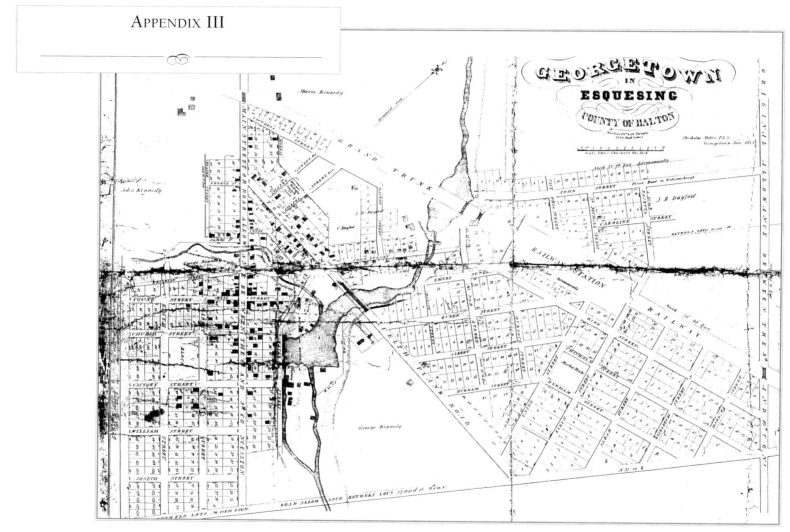

Plan of Georgetown, 1854

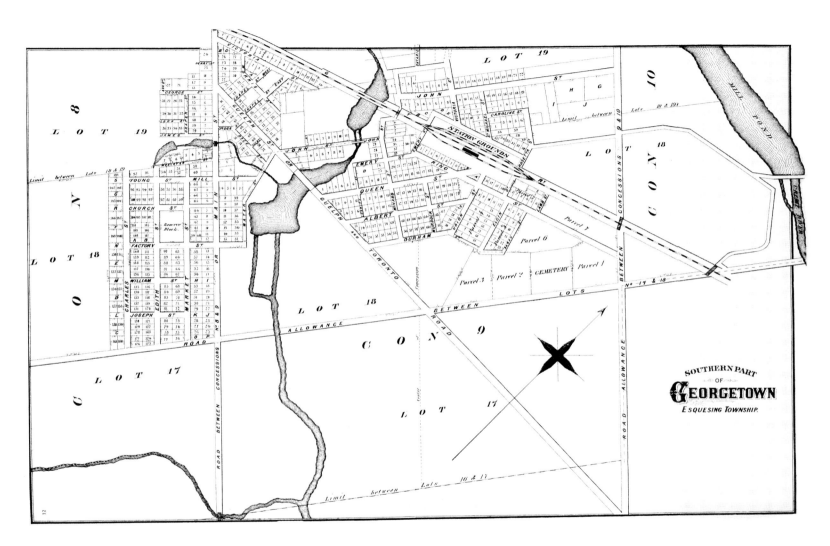

Map of Georgetown, 1877. Taken from the *Historical Atlas of Halton County,* 1877.

BIBLIOGRAPHY

BOOKS & REPORTS

Archaeological Resource Assessment, Mayer Heritage Consultants Ltd, June 1992.

Archival Papers, Vol I, John Mark Rowe, Ed., Esquesing Historical Society, 1990. *Barber Paper Mill Designation Report*, John Mark Rowe, Heritage Halton Hills, 2004.

Life & Writings, Arthur Charles Dayfoot, Toronto:2002

Account Book 1860–1862, John B. Dayfoot, Esquesing Historical Society Archives, Georgetown.

Daybook 1868–1869, P.W. Dayfoot, Esquesing Historical Society Archives, Georgetown, Dayfoot Collection.

Constitution of the Georgetown, Esquesing, Union Sunday School Society, MS, Esquesing Historical Society Archives, Georgetown: 1843.

Sacred Feathers, Donald B. Smith, Toronto: 1987.

"Georgetown Wesleyan Methodist Cemetery" Elaine Robinson Bertrand, *Archaeological Resource Assessment*, Mayer Heritage Consultants Ltd, June: 1992.

Numbering The Survivors, J. Richard Houston, 1979.

Religious Development in Esquesing Township 1819–1900, Richard E. Ruggle, PhD MS, Toronto: 1990.

Directory of Georgetown in 1856, provided by Lachlan Grant, *The Georgetown Herald*, 5 March 1924.

Fuller's Directory of Halton and Peel for 1866–1867.

Halton Sketches, John McDonald, Georgetown: 1976.

Halton Sketches Revisited, John McDonald, Norval: 1996.

Halton Pages of the Past, Gwen Clarke, Acton: 1955.

"Maple Leaf Dairy", Norma Thompson, undated MS.

Memorandum to John Mark Rowe from James F. Kidd, Manuscript Division, Archives of Canada, 21 September 1993.

St. George's Anglican Church, A History, Richard E. Ruggle, Georgetown:1982.

Knox Presbyterian Church, Georgetown, Ontario, Janet McDougall et. al., Georgetown:1960.

"Georgetown District High School", Thompson Ramautarsingh, *GDHS Centennial Book 1887–1987*

Private Education in Georgetown, John Mark Benbow Rowe, Georgetown: 1988.

Nelson Burns His Autobiography, "Evolution of the Gospel of Mr. Burns" *The Expositor of the Christ–Life*, Toronto: Vol.65, No. 3, September 1967.

Historic Railway Stations report No. 216 on Georgetown VIA Rail Station, August 1994.

North Halton Golf and Country Club, Janet Duval, Georgetown: 2003.

The Diamond Plateau 1928–1988, The Royal Canadian Legion Branch 120, Georgetown: 1988.

Reminiscences of Jean Ruddell, Esquesing Historical Society meeting of 10 May 1995.

John McDonald, Esquesing Historical Society meeting, 9 February 2005.

NEWSPAPERS

The Daily Leader, Toronto, 25 March 1854.

The British Whig, Kingston, 13 October 1847

The Hamilton Spectator

The Guelph Advertiser

The Streetsville Review

Toronto Daily Mail, 1893

The Canadian Champion, (Georgetown) Milton.

The Halton Herald, Georgetown

The Acton Free Press

The New Tanner, Acton

The Georgetown (Halton Hills) Herald

The Georgetown Leader

The Georgetown Independent

PUBLISHED ARTICLES

"Justices of the Peace" Richard E. Ruggle, *The Herald,* 30 January 1985.

"Our Town's First Post Office", Richard E. Ruggle, *Halton Hills Herald,*
5 June 1985.

"A Tour to the West", Viator, *British Whig,* Kingston, 13 October 1847

"Dayfoots Come to Georgetown", Rev. Rick Ruggle, *The Herald,*
22 August 1984

"Opening of the Trafalgar, Esquesing and Erin Road", *The Hamilton
Spectator,* 7 December 1850.

"The Plank Road Ball", *The Hamilton Spectator,* 16 January 1851;
The Guelph Advertiser, 31 January 1850.

Editorial columns by William Glass Stewart, *The Hamilton Spectator,*
17 March 1854.

"The Georgetown Star", *The Streetsville Review,* 20 May 1854.

"Thriving Holy Cross Parish has evolved from backwoods mission"
John Mark Rowe, *The Independent, Georgetown,* 14 November 1984.

"Beginnings of militia go back to settlers", Rev. Rick Ruggle,
The Independent, Georgetown, 7 October 1987.

Acton Free Press, 31 March 1892.

"Georgetown's second Reeve", Rev. Rick Ruggle, *Georgetown Herald,*
11 July 1984; "William McLeod and the Mammoth House", Rev. Rick
Ruggle, *Georgetown Herald,* 18 July 1984.

"Library started as Mechanics Institute", Walter Lewis, *Esquesing Historical
Society Collections,* Volume 1: 1984.

"Long Military Tradition continues with Lorne Scots", Rev. Rick Ruggle,
Georgetown Independent, 10 November 1983.

"Beginning of Knox Church", *The Independent, Georgetown,*
13 November 1985.

"Creelman – A Big Name in Knitting Machines", Anne Lindsay,
Georgetown Independent, 2 October 1985

"Odd Fellows Here 100 Years", Elaine Robinson–Bertrand, *Collections One,*
Esquesing Historical Society 1984.

"Reminiscences of Georgetown", C.W. Young, *Georgetown Herald,*
3 July 1940

"Georgetown College", *Acton Free Press,* 28 August 1878.

"1889 — A Dream Year for Georgetown Educators", John Mark Rowe,
Halton Hills Herald, 4 June 1986.

"Its been half a century but 39s royal tour remembered" Hartley Coles,
Georgetown Independent, 1989.

"Halton Boys off for South Africa" *Acton Free Press,* 11 January 1900.

"Georgetown Herald Destroyed last Thursday" *Acton Free Press,*
2 May 1918

"1884 marks beginning of Bell's 'social chats'", Walter Lewis,
Halton Hills Herald, 1983.

"Paper Mills Run by Electricity", *Acton Free Press,* 5 September 1889

"Independent Order of Good Templars", Stephen Dafoe,
http://www.templarhistory.com/goodtemplars.html, 23 January 2005.

"1997 Georgetown Hockey Council Citation Recipients"
http://www.gmha.on.ca/1997.htm, 31 March 2005.

"A Brief History of St. John's"
http://www.stjohnsuc.ca/aboutus.html, 31 January 2005.

CONTRIBUTING INDIVIDUALS

Keith Barber

Marie Beaumont

Tudor Beaumont

Bud Bishop

Betty Brownridge

Luena Campbell

Barry Canon

Geoff Canon

Frank Chisholm

Doug Cole

Arthur Dayfoot

Kathy Gastle

Gord Graham

Mary Barber Findley

Bruce Harding

George Henderson

Dorothy Hill

Elmer Hill

Karen Hunter

Rick Hunter

Frank M. Kennedy

Jean Layman

Walter Lewis

Dawn Livingstone

Jack Livingstone

Marion Lookman

Bill McDonald

John McDonald

Marshall Neilson

Allan Norton

Russell Miller

Gord Preston

Elaine Robinson

Jean Ruddell

Richard Ruggle

Ine Sargent

George Sargent

Arthur Speight

Elsie Weaver

Fanny Weaver

Fred Weaver

Una Wheeler

Marion Van Wyck

The Story of Georgetown
is *autographed by author*
John Mark Rowe for
Teresa and Ken Lamb of the
Milton Historical Society.
Halton Hills This Week,
17 October 1992

Georgetown librarians Geoff Cannon and Walter Lewis display
the new computer dial-up access introduced to Halton Hills
Public Libraries. Halton Hills This Week,, 28 October 1992

INDEX

ESQUESING HISTORICAL SOCIETY

The Region of Halton is a compact little county, bounded on the north by Wellington County, on the south by Lake Ontario, on the east by Peel Region, and on the west by Hamilton–Wentworth Region. It is made up of four townships: Esquesing, Nassagaweya, Nelson and Trafalgar. Our particular area of interest is Esquesing.

The Esquesing Historical Society was founded on January 1, 1975, and is named after the geographical township called Esquesing, most of which encompasses the present Corporation of the Town of Halton Hills. In 1986 we were incorporated through our affiliation with the Ontario Historical Society.

It is the mandate of the Esquesing Historical Society to educate the public about the history of our area, and we try to do this by holding our meetings at various places around the township, as they might pertain to the meeting subject. We are also charged with collecting, preserving and disseminating information about our area. From time to time, the Society publishes books of local history.

Our mandate was given a boost by agreement in 1982 with the Halton Hills Public Libraries which enabled the Society to establish archives in the Georgetown branch. Since that time the Library has been our most stalwart supporter.

The Historical Society maintains an ever increasing collection of archival material and photographs, housed in the Georgetown Branch of Halton Hills Public Libraries. These are all indexed, filed, and preserved in archival acid free containers. The Archives are becoming an ever increasing source for local history. The collection is available to the public on a request basis, and information on the collection can be found at the library, in the reference department, or searched on the society's website — www.esquesinghistoricalsociety.ca .

Presidents of the Esquesing Historical Society have been John McDonald, Steamer Emmerson, George Henderson, Rev. Rick Ruggle, Elaine Robinson, John Mark Rowe, Sherry Halliday, Karen Hunter and Steve Blake.

Membership in the Esquesing Historical Society entitles the member to receive informative newsletters, attend our meetings and allows a discount on all society publications. All meetings are open and free to the public.